THE FOOD & COOKING OF
PAKISTAN

THE FOOD & COOKING OF PAKISTAN

TRADITIONAL DISHES FROM THE HOME KITCHEN

SHEHZAD HUSAIN

LORENZ BOOKS

BONUS
BONUS
BONUS
ISO
Wt.
Wt
40 Kg

CONTENTS

PAKISTANI CUISINE

Nestled between four distinct and diverse nations – Afghanistan, China, India and Iran – Pakistan is a melting pot of influences and home to some of the best food on the planet. Whether you purchase a sizzling kebab from a ramshackle streetside stall or sit down to a formal meal comprising a wide range of delectable aromatic dishes, the careful combinations of ingredients are sure to entice you back for more.

Geographically, Pakistan can be roughly divided into three: the vertiginous northern parts, home to the Himalayas and such extensive glaciers that the region is often dubbed the 'third Pole'; the Indus River plain, the fertile heartland where the majority of the population resides; and the Sistan basin, an arid, mountainous zone that is prone to earthquakes.

Part of India until Partition in 1947, the lines that delineate Pakistan's borders have long been a source of conflict, with the region of Kashmir in particular being hotly contested. Various passes and corridors, including the Khyber Pass, allow access to neighbouring countries, and cross-cultural trends are especially evident in these regions.

LOCAL INGREDIENTS

The terrain and climate of much of Pakistan are not conducive to food production, with limited water supplies, fairly poor soil and often freezing temperatures in rocky mountain ranges and blistering heat in arid desert zones. The vast majority of the nation's nourishment comes from the Indus region, and it is here that the two major provinces, Punjab and Sindh, are located. On the floodplain of one of the world's greatest rivers, the Indus, sultry mangrove swamps and freshwater tributaries teeming with shrimp lie next to rigorously irrigated arable land that produces a range of crops, from wheat, rice and pulses to sugarcane, cotton and vegetables.

Lamb and chicken are by far and away the most popular forms of protein in this Muslim nation, alongside goat and mutton, although beef is occasionally eaten. Fish from the 800km-long (500 mile-long) coastline is a less common feature on menus, although juicy prawns from the inland waterways are widely enjoyed. Vegetarian food is not especially common, although pulses and vegetables are incorporated into many recipes and the tradition of serving lots of different dishes at each meal means that a daal or a vegetable accompaniment is usually present.

REGIONAL SPECIALITIES

Pakistani food is a blend of several culinary traditions, including those of Afghanistan, Iran, Persia, the West and China, as well as of course India, of which Pakistan was once part. Mughlai cooking – typified by its use of herbs, spices, almonds and dried fruit – is the dominant style upon which Pakistani recipes are based, forming a gastronomic link with Uttar Pradesh, Delhi and Hyderabad in northern India. In addition to these centuries-old classics, dishes known for their richness and flavour have been created since

BELOW Pakistan has total land area of about 800,000 square kilometres (500,000 square miles), and extends from mountain ranges in the north to the Arabian Sea in the south.

ABOVE A land of contrasts, Pakistan features thickly forested mountain ranges, arid desert zones, lush delta plains and mosque-studded skylines.

Independence in 1947 and can be categorized as 'Lahori' or 'Pakistani' cuisine today. Outside Pakistan, restaurants are increasingly featuring 'Lahori' or 'Peshawari' cuisine, although the classification is often blurred by the establishments' use of the generic description 'Indian restaurant', masking the food's true origins.

Back in Pakistan, more distinct regional differences are to be found. For instance, Punjab is famous for its roti and elaborate, highly seasoned dishes, whereas in the nearby coastal Sindh province, machli (fish) and shellfish feature more. Farther west near the border with Afghanistan, Pashtun and Balochi cuisines tend not to be as spiced, the former featuring many rice dishes alongside kebabs and the latter being the home of the sajji method of cooking whole lambs on skewers in a pit over hot coals. Peshawari cuisine features large chunks of lightly spiced marinated meat, fish and vegetables that are often slow-cooked in a clay tandoor oven, which imbues the food with an inimitable smokiness. While the ingredients tend to be simple and the spice selection small, the preparation is precise, the aim being to bring the very best out of each and every ingredient.

Of course, home-cooked food inevitably varies from household to household, with cooks tweaking and adapting traditional recipes as well as exploring foreign cuisines. In recent years, many European, American and, in particular, Chinese restaurants have become increasingly popular, especially in the larger cities. Consequently, most urban households now include pasta, pizzas, roasts, hamburgers, chops, salads, pies, cakes and Western desserts in their culinary repertoire. Chinese food is so beloved that a distinct Pakistani-style Chinese cuisine has evolved, featuring fusion dishes such as Chinese-style samosas and pulaos. Almost as popular is Thai food, and it has become a tradition in many households to frequently make and serve a range of both Chinese and Thai dishes, particularly at the often rather competitive ladies' luncheon gatherings.

KARACHI TO LAHORE – PAKISTAN'S URBAN HUBS

Dubbed the 'city that never sleeps', the Sindhi capital Karachi is one of the most populated cities in the world and is (in)famous for its lively night life, massive shopping malls and the largest food street in Asia, the Port Grand Food and Entertainment Complex. The site of most of the nation's key business, education, culture, arts, fashion and other industries, this major port city is a melting pot of different groups from all over Pakistan as well as migrants from South Asia, although Islam is very much the dominant religion and culture. It is here that food trends from around the world are introduced to and assimilated into the country's cuisine, as well as

THE ROLE OF ISLAM

Islam has been the predominant religion in the region since the 7th century AD and today it is the state religion, with the majority of people practising Sunni Islam. This brings with it certain rules about how and what food can be eaten – no pork can be consumed, meat must be halal and prepared in a very specific way, no alcohol is permitted – as well as many wonderful celebratory dishes that are served at the various festivals that occur throughout the year.

In addition to the available ingredients, religion has played a major role in shaping the country's eating habits as well as the dishes that are placed upon the table. During the Islamic holy month of Ramadan, it is not permitted for Muslims to eat or drink anything between sunrise and sunset, and the eating patterns change to sehri (a pre-dawn meal) and iftar (the sunset break of fast). It is customary to break the fast with the consumption of a single date and a vivifying rose-syrup drink, followed by all manner of nourishing dishes.These special mealtimes are very communal and lively occasions, with a wide range of foods and thirst-quenching drinks cooked and served en-masse, and friends and family coming together. In mosques, food is set out in neat rows and is provided for everybody, from the richest to the poorest.

providing the many foreigners there on business or for the pleasure of visiting the city's beaches, museums, bazaars and historic buildings with authentic Muhajir (a term used to describe Muslim immigrants and their descendants of multi-ethnic origin) food. Biryanis are among the city's keynote dishes, alongside bun kebabs, kat-a-kat chicken and nehari, the nation's favourite dish.

The capital, Islamabad, is situated on the opposite side of the country, and was built in the 1960s in order to balance out the dominance of the former capital Karachi. Today, it is a thriving business and higher-education centre and the seat of the nation's government. Although the city is relatively new, the Potohar Plateau on which it is situated is one of the earliest sites of human settlement in Asia, with relics dating back 7,000 years to Neolithic times. Neighbouring Rawalpindi, an ancient Gakhar city with which Islamabad is twinned, is also steeped in history, and it is believed that it was home to a distinct cultural group as far back as 1,000BCE, with remains showing that the region's religion was once Buddhism. In much more recent times, the city became the most important cantonment of the entire British Raj in the mid 19th century. It was during this time that numerous British culinary trends – such as the tradition of teatime and various Western cakes, pastries and other delicacies – were often embraced, albeit with a spicy Asian twist.

Lahore, the capital of Punjab province and the second-largest city, is widely considered to be the seat of the nation's cultural, historical and intellectual jewels. From Mughal forts and grand mosques to Colonial relics and ancient tombs, the city resonates with history and has a distinct and rich food culture that is celebrated elsewhere in Pakistan as well as abroad. Seekh kebabs, haleem and gol gappay are just some of the dishes for which the city is famous.

RURAL LIFE

Most people outside the massive urban hubs live in very traditional villages, often in houses made from bricks, clay or mud (or even interlinked caves in one region of Balochistan), and with several generations of the same family cohabiting under the same roof. Farming, and in particular the rearing of livestock, is the dominant industry in the often harsh landscape, although associated trades such as blacksmithing and shepherding are options.

The food in these areas tends to be more simple than that found in the cities, with dishes featuring local ingredients and employing age-old techniques, such as tandoori cooking and the roasting of kebabs over hot coals. Conditions can be tough, and wheat and rice are the staple foods, alongside meat, dairy, and whatever vegetables and fruit can be produced. This has resulted in localized cuisines, dominated by bread and rice, but often surprisingly sophisticated in taste thanks to the judicious and experienced use of spices and aromatic ingredients.

PAKISTANI GASTRONOMY

People customarily eat three meals a day in Pakistan (apart from during Ramadan), namely breakfast, lunch and dinner, although street snacks and high tea are popular too. It is traditional for the lady of the house to shop for fresh ingredients daily and prepare all the meals from scratch, although as working hours for men and women increase and time for cooking is at ever more of a premium, Pakistanis are more often turning to convenience foods – in particular ready-blended spices and store-bought breads and pastries – and fast food is extremely popular.

Fortunately, the range of street food on offer is as delicious as it is diverse, from sizzlingly aromatic kebabs and an array of chaat (snacks) to freshly baked breads, pastries and sweetmeats and a

LEFT Traditionally, the woman of the house in Pakistan goes shopping for fresh ingredients on a daily basis and cooks meals from scratch.

BOTTOM LEFT Farming is the dominant profession among rural people in Pakistan, with wheat being the most important national crop.

BELOW Hardy goats and sheep are a main source of milk, meat and skins in often-harsh environments.

BOTTOM Fish are an important part of the daily diets of those who live by the coast or the many inland waterways, including Lake Manchar, the largest freshwater lake in Pakistan and one of the biggest in the whole of Asia.

tempting array of fresh fruit, all sold from ramshackle streetside hawker stalls as well as at more permanent eateries.

Breakfast is a proper meal for many – no anaemic toast and soggy cereal here: Pakistanis put fire in their bellies right from the off with nutritious chickpea dishes, substantial omelettes, spiced qeema (ground meat) dishes such as nehari (the name of which translates as 'day break'), as well as breads, seasonal fruits, cheese-filled pastries and many more regional delicacies, all washed down with cups of strong chai or a soothing and substantial lassi.

Lunch is an equally good spread when eaten at home, usually featuring goat, lamb or beef curry cooked with spinach, potatoes or daal, and served with steamed rice or a roti of some kind. There are always accompaniments of Pakistani salad, raita, spicy pickles and chutneys at the table too. People who live near rivers often enjoy fish for lunch, perhaps cooked in the tandoori style, while office workers may just pop to a nearby food stand for a steaming bowl of lentil or meat stew and a fresh roti or chapati, eaten with the fingers while sitting cross-legged on a raised platform called a takht. During the sultry summer months, those who are not out at work commonly take a siesta after lunch to avoid the worst of the intense heat and digest the meal at leisure.

Dinner, usually the main meal of the day and often eaten quite late during the cool of the evening, typically consists of some curry or qorma with perhaps kebabs, a salad, and a daal or vegetable curry, and is invariably served with roti or rice. Daal chawal (lentils with rice) is another favourite accompaniment, as are papar (poppadums), which are freshly fried or lightly grilled or broiled and served with the meal – not as an appetizer, as is the custom in many 'Indian' restaurants in the West. The latter tend to be bought ready-to-fry rather than being made from scratch.

While not necessarily a daily feature, desserts are included on the menu in many homes, especially if there are guests present. These often consist of tempting platters of attractively prepared seasonal fresh fruit, such as mangoes and melons, and one or two other desserts, such as kheer (rice pudding) or a variety of sweetmeats, such as gulab jamun or ras malai, bought from one of the many sweet stores or itinerant vendors that are found in most neighbourhoods.

As alcohol is forbidden, chilled or iced water is always served at all meals, together with a selection of carbonated drinks, fresh fruit juices (such as mango, watermelon or orange), and sometimes shikanjabeen (an uplifting drink made from the juice of tiny lemons combined with sugar, mint leaves and crushed ice), limu pani (similar to shikanjabeen, but made with limes), or the invigorating sweet or mango lassi. To round off the meal, tea is always served, and it was once customary to offer paan (a small betel leaf wrap containing betel nuts, cardamoms, shredded dried coconut and sometimes tobacco), although since it came to light that betel could cause cancer, this habit is now less common. On the street, freshly squeezed fruit juices such as orange, pomegranate and sugarcane are particular favourites at the many pop-up stalls and stores that line the bustling streets – nutritious and enlivening thirst-quenchers at any time of the day.

OPPOSITE TOP Sweet-sellers are a common, and very welcome, sight in Pakistan's cities, parading the streets and beaches with their bright wares balanced expertly on their heads.

OPPOSITE BOTTOM Dining out at restaurants and in smart hotels is a popular pastime among the affluent classes, whether for a main meal or the ever-popular high tea.

OPPOSITE BOTTOM Fruit juices, water and carbonated drinks are served with every meal and are also sold from hawker carts and stalls on the streets.

TIME FOR TEA

Dating back to the time of the Raj, high tea is a tradition that has been wholeheartedly embraced by certain echelons of Pakistani society, and is offered in well-to-do homes as well as smart hotels and restaurants. A buffet-style meal, it usually includes a selection of savoury snacks, such as patties made of puff pastry stuffed with spiced ground lamb or chicken, chicken wings, kebabs, fruit chaat and potato fries, followed by several types of Western-style (and extremely popular) cakes and pastries, such as cupcakes and lemon tarts. This is all washed down with, of course, copious amounts of strong chai or tea.

Tea is drunk socially more or less throughout the day in Pakistan and is offered to every visitor, whether in the house or at the office. It can be made the usual way in a teapot with boiling water, or with hot milk that is heated in a pan over a low heat with tea leaves, cardamom and sugar. Green tea has become increasingly favoured of late, especially among the bright young things in the cities. Given this penchant, it is no surprise that skilled chai-wallahs are a ubiquitous sight on every street corner, station and thoroughfare in the country, deftly pouring steaming streams of fragrant tea from great heights into chipped enamel cups for the delectation of the thirsty customer.

FESTIVALS & CELEBRATIONS

Pakistanis love a party, especially when food is involved (as it nearly always is), so it is fortunate that the national and religious calendar offers so many opportunities for lavish get-togethers to occur. Apart from the national commemorative days, Pakistanis celebrate many religious events and occasions, namely the birthday of the Prophet; Eid al-Fitr; Eid al-Adha and many others.

Each festive occasion in Pakistan is marked by people getting together, socializing, meeting, greeting and offering blessings or mubaraks to each other. The focus of each occasion, alongside prayer, tends to be feasting on special meals, sweet treats and snacks, with the many different foods laid out buffet-style.

EID AL-FITR

The highlight of the Islamic calendar is Eid al-Fitr, which falls on the first day of the lunar month following the holy month of Ramadan. I remember as a child looking forward to Eid and becoming very excited during the preparations, which centred on shopping for the big day, when we would don new clothes and both receive and visit friends and relations. It is a particularly special day for all the children as they receive Eidi (presents, traditionally money) from the elders, and enjoy all the fuss and food.

Almost as important as the big day itself is the night before Eid, known as Chand Raat. This is when the new moon is sighted, heralding the start of the Eid festivities and causing a flurry of excitement and activity with most stores remaining open late to cater to last-minute shoppers looking for vibrant bangles for the girls and shoes and clothing for all. Females visit henna booths or invite experts to their homes to decorate their palms with intricately patterned designs. Street stores and cafés selling fast food and snacks do a roaring trade. At home, there is a party atmosphere with youngsters singing and dancing to uplifting music and gorging themselves on the various foods.

Eid day begins early in the morning, when the menfolk dress up in crisp and new national dress – the shalwar and kurta – and congregate to listen to the sermon and offer Eid prayers in a dedicated open area or the local mosque. Before the Eid prayer, Muslims are obligated to pay Zakat al-Fitr, a charity donation that goes to poorer families who cannot otherwise engage in the occasion. After prayers, the men congratulate each other and go home to join in the festivities with the whole family and enjoy the elaborate Eid breakfast, which mainly consists of sweet dishes such as sheer qorma or seviyan (a rich milk-based dessert made with broken vermicelli), dates and other sweetmeats. These are on offer for drop-in guests throughout the day, giving rise to the nickname 'sweet Eid' for this happy finale to Ramadan. The day of feasting culminates with a meal of biryani, numerous curries, breads, salads, kebabs, raita, seviyan or other milk-based desserts, and fresh fruit.

EID AL-ADHA

The other major event is Eid al-Adha (the festival of sacrifice) – in Pakistan known as Baqr-'Eid, literally 'the greater Eid' – and celebrated the day after the very important Hajj pilgrimage in Mecca. Hajj lasts for 10 days and is performed each year by millions of Muslim pilgrims to commemorate the sacrificial offering of a ram by the Prophet Abraham. Hajj is obligatory for every able Muslim and is performed in the tradition of Prophet Mohammad, involving regular prayers and circumambulation (tawaf) at Islam's holiest site, the Ka'aba. In addition, the pilgrimage also includes a trip to Islam's second-holiest shrine, the Mosque of the Prophet in the city of Madinah, where the Holy Prophet and two of his companions are buried. Both the mosques in Mecca and Madinah are spectacularly beautiful and are visited by millions of pilgrims and worshippers not just at Hajj but throughout the year.

BELOW Women congregate to offer Salat al-Eid (prayers) in a mosque in Lahore during Eid al-Adha. Males and females worship separately before coming together to celebrate and feast.

ABOVE Many favourite dishes are served buffet-style at big celebrations so that everyone can help themselves. Sweetmeats and desserts are on offer throughout the day for guests and visitors.

Like all Muslim religious festivals, Eid al-Adha begins with prayers. All the menfolk (and sometimes the women, separately) congregate early in the morning in a mosque or an eidgah – an open-air gathering place usually outside the city or at the outskirts – to perform Salat al-Eid (Eid prayers). After this the families get together at home.

Eid al-Adha is a joyous occasion when everyone dresses up in new clothes. The festivities last for four days, during which time a lamb, goat or cow is slaughtered to commemorate the Prophet Abraham's readiness to sacrifice his son. Two-thirds of the meat is distributed among family, friends and the poor. A third portion is for personal consumption and is used to cook delectable dishes, such as spiced fried kidneys, nehari, haleem, pasanda qorma, shami kebabs and biryanis, to name but a few. Most households have an open-house buffet feast set out, to which all visitors who come to wish 'Eid Mubarak' are invited to help themselves. A separate table laden with lavish desserts, such as seviyan, sweetmeats and fresh fruit is also prepared.

EID MILAD-UN-NABI

The Prophet Muhammad's birthday, Eid Milad-un-Nabi, is celebrated on different dates of the third month of the Islamic calendar, Rabi-ul-Awwal, by Shia and Sunni Muslims. The occasion is generally celebrated throughout the Islamic world with gun salutes, the national flag being flown at full mast, and mosques, streets and public buildings being decorated and illuminated. In Pakistan, prayers, blessing and incantations in praise of the Holy Prophet are offered up. The celebrations also include private feasts and the distribution of sweetmeats and food to the poor and needy at mosques.

SHAB-E-BARAT

The next festival in the Islamic calendar is Shab-e-barat, or 'Night of Innocence', which commemorates the entry of the Prophet into the city of Mecca and is marked by a night of prayer. Considered one of the holiest nights in the Islamic calendar, it is celebrated with a display of fireworks. Every household prepares halwas and Pakistani sweetmeats for friends and family, as well as the poor.

WEDDINGS

Pakistani weddings are very big affairs, with guest lists ranging from 200 to 2,000 people. They are usually fairly elaborate and the celebrations can last for up to a week, during which time an open-house policy is observed at the home of the bride. Each night, mostly women gather there and perform dances to Bollywood music or 'Bhangra' – typical Punjabi dances performed to Pakistani music. Henna is applied on the bride and her friends and family, and this is followed by dinner, which can vary from barbecues featuring kebabs and other meats to halwa puri with chana masala. Sometimes there are stalls set up in the garden, which are laden with dishes from various other favourite cuisines, such as Chinese, Thai or Lebanese.

The Nikah ceremony, which is the actual wedding, takes place either on a large lawn or in a big hotel. A lavish banquet spread will be on offer, featuring a biryani and a pulao of some sort, as well as a chicken or mutton qorma, makhani or palak, salads, breads, rice, and desserts such as gajar ka halwa, kheer and zarda.

THE PAKISTANI KITCHEN

A traditional Pakistani kitchen consists of little more than a fire, over which meat can be grilled or broiled, thin flatbreads can be cooked on a hotplate, and all manner of delectable curries can be stewed in a heavy pan. In the Northwest Frontier Province (and sometimes elsewhere) a tandoor or clay oven is also used, whether communally or in individual households, although of course many Pakistani homes today are fully equipped with modern appliances. Classic ingredients are similarly simple, with many recipes featuring the same few foods – such as ginger, garlic, onions, chana masala – in varying combinations and quantities, and it is this careful blending that differentiates the dishes both from each other and those of other South Asian cuisines.

TOOLS AND EQUIPMENT

Your own kitchen will probably already be equipped with the majority of the cooking equipment required for making the recipes in this book: a few good-quality pans with thick bases and a heavy frying pan or skillet will take you a long way. In addition, you will need some wooden spatulas and, ideally, a slotted spoon for stirring and separating rice grains. You should have at least one decent sharp knife and, for measuring, some spoons, a measuring jug or cup, and a set of kitchen scales.

For grinding spices you can use a pestle and mortar, a coffee grinder or food processor, or a rolling pin. In many Pakistani households, a flat, heavy grindstone and a mussal (similar to a rolling pin) are still considered the best implements for the job.

In a typical Pakistani kitchen you would probably find a tawa, which is a cast-iron frying pan used for cooking chapatis and parathas and for roasting spices; a karahi – an aluminium or stainless-steel pan used for deep-frying, which resembles a straight-sided wok with handles on either side; and possibly a girda – a small (25cm/10in-diameter) pastry board on short legs, which is used for rolling out dough. However, many people now use a clean kitchen worktop instead. Electronic rice cookers are also popular throughout the East wherever rice is cooked regularly and in large quantities, and Pakistan is no exception. It ensures perfectly cooked rice every time, which is kept warm until required, and is easy to clean.

If you have a pressure cooker you might well find it useful: it will certainly reduce the cooking time for large joints of lamb or beef. Whether using a pressure cooker or a slow cooker, you must brown the onions first and stir-fry the meat and spices briefly before transferring the mixture to the cooker (this will improve flavour and colour). As a rule, cook the food until the surplus liquid has been completely absorbed. In the case of a pressure cooker, you can remove the lid for this final stage. You will also find a pressure cooker useful for cooking daals, some of which (depending, very often, on how old they are) can take a long time to tenderize.

When you are planning a Pakistani feast, a freezer is invaluable. If I am making a big dinner, I usually start preparing about a week to ten days in advance (two or three days beforehand is ample time for a small gathering) and freeze the dishes as I make them. All the kebabs and the majority of the curries in this book freeze beautifully, whether made with meat or without. There is one vegetable, however, that becomes mushy when cooked and frozen, namely the potato. So if you intend to freeze a dish that contains potato, omit it from the initial cooking and add it to the thawed dish on the day it will be served.

LEFT A hotplate, a few karahis and some basic tools and utensils are the most important cooking implements in a simple traditional Pakistani kitchen, such as this one in Chitral.

To reheat thawed food, either place it in the oven in a covered pan or heatproof serving dish, or under a low grill or broiler, depending on the type of dish; you could also shallow-fry it if it is something with a sauce, but I find this makes things a little greasy. A microwave oven is of course another way of thawing and reheating frozen dishes, but check carefully how much time you will need to allow in order to cope with all the different items, since a microwave's capacity is restricted. You should also consider how you plan to keep things warm as you heat them one by one – using an oven to heat multiple dishes at once, reserving the microwave just for items that heat quickly, such as rice, may be the best way to proceed.

Finally, do not forget that if you have a hostess trolley this too can be very useful when entertaining Pakistani-style. As well as enabling you to keep all of the different dishes hot until the moment you put them on the table, you won't spend the evening endlessly darting backwards and forwards into the kitchen, since everything will be ready to hand in one place. Using one will even allow you time, if you wish, to clear up the kitchen before your guests arrive. If you don't have a trolley, it is a good idea to put the dishes on several large trays.

ABOVE Everyday spices are often stored in beautiful wooden spice boxes.

BELOW Traditional Pakistani kebabs are formed around thick metal skewers, while karahis, which can be made from metals such as aluminium, stainless steel or copper, are used for frying foods.

KEY INGREDIENTS

Pakistani dishes rely on the quality and freshness of the simple ingredients that go into their making, for their elevation to excellence. Aromatics such as onions, garlic, ginger, chillies and fresh herbs lift the flavour base supplied by the primary ingredient – be it lamb, beef, lentils, rice or potatoes – and together with the clever combinations of spices imbue the food with an unforgettable flavour.

STORECUPBOARD STAPLES Your basic stock of dried spices should include ground chilli powder, turmeric, cardamom, black pepper, coriander and cumin. The powdered spices will keep well in carefully labelled airtight containers or spice jars, although in Pakistan they would traditionally be stored in beautiful decorated wooden spice boxes. Other useful spices to have on hand include: whole cumin seeds

ABOVE, LEFT TO RIGHT Garlic, fresh root ginger and many types of fresh herbs are key ingredients in many dishes.

(black and white), onion seeds, mustard seeds, cloves, cinnamon sticks, dried chillies, fenugreek and garam masala, the latter of which is a blend usually consisting of green and black cardamom pods, cinnamon, cloves, peppercorns and mace. Chaat masala (a mix of dried mango powder, ground coriander, cumin and ginger, chilli powder, salt, pepper and asafoetida) is also invaluable for adding zing to roasted and fried foods, and salads.

FRESH PRODUCE The range of indigenous vegetables and fruits available in Pakistan is relatively small when compared with the incredible array on offer in modern Western stores, to which many Pakistanis, and especially those living in rural parts, would never have access. Potatoes, onions, garlic, ginger, chillies, cauliflowers, spinach, okra, tomatoes and aubergines or eggplants as well as chickpeas and various types of lentil (chana, masoor, yellow, split) are the primary vegetables that recur in traditional dishes. These, alongside fresh herbs, bring colour and flavour as well as nutritional benefits to the everyday diet.

Fresh fruits are mostly of the tropical variety, with dates, mangoes, papaya, lemons and limes especially popular in desserts and beverages such as lassis and limu pani (lemonade). Papaya, in addition to being enjoyed raw, is employed as a tenderizing agent that breaks down meat proteins during marinating. Nuts – pistachios, almonds, cashews, pine nuts and walnuts – are both eaten raw and used in cooking, lending taste, texture and protein to curries, rice dishes, desserts, drinks and sweetmeats.

HOW TO PREPARE GINGER PULP AND GARLIC PULP

As ginger and garlic pulps take time and effort to prepare, and appear so frequently in Pakistani cuisine, I suggest that you make big batches. Take about 200g/8oz of each and soak overnight in a bowl of cold water (this makes them easy to peel). The next day, peel off the skin and grind them, separately, in a food processor, adding a little water to form a pulp. These can be stored in an airtight container in a cool place for a month or longer, or poured into ice-cube trays and frozen as individual portions that thaw very quickly.

Meat and poultry play a key role in the daily diets of many Pakistanis – far more so than in most South Asian cuisines – although poorer families consume less than those who are better off. Sheep and goats, those hardy itinerant creatures, are perhaps the nation's favourite, although beef is also enjoyed. Pork is, of course, forbidden for Muslims. Having been butchered in accordance with Islamic law, the halal meat is usually diced into cubes to be simmered in a sauce or finely ground and used for making kebabs or queema, and Pakistan is unusual for the manner in which it combines meat with lentils. Chickens (and their eggs) are almost as popular as lamb, their tender meat being the ideal carrier for subtle spice combinations and obligingly versatile when it comes to cooking; whether marinated, skewered and cooked on a barbecue or in a tandoor, steamed, stir-fried or simmered in a sauce, chicken always tastes good.

Fish and seafood are less common features on menus away from the coast, although prawns (shrimp) are widely enjoyed everywhere, especially in side dishes or light meals.

ABOVE Qulfi, here being made and sold on the street, is one of many milk-based treats in Pakistan.

Dairy, most notably milk, cream, yogurt and ghee, appears in numerous dishes, especially the milk desserts that are so beloved at Eid, namely seviyan, kheer, qulfi and gulab jamun. These classics were originally conceived of as a means of using up milk before it went off, transforming a product that would rapidly spoil into a delicacy with a longer shelf life. Cream was made for the same reason, the day's unpasteurized milk being boiled on a stove all afternoon before the thick cream that rose to the surface was scooped off and added to similarly slow-cooked curries. Yogurt, yet another product of milk preservation, appears in drinks and curries, where it is whisked with spices and used as a tenderizing marinade or added at the end to lend creaminess to a curry, as well as for the ubiquitous raita. Pakistani yogurt is thick and full-fat, important factors both for the texture and flavour this adds to a dish and also because lower-fat products split more easily. Greek (US strained plain) yogurt is the best alternative outside Pakistan, and it helps if you whisk it with a fork before blending it with other ingredients.

Ghee has long been a popular cooking fat in Pakistan, though some people now prefer to use the slightly healthier version made from vegetable fat rather than the more traditional type made from pure butterfat.

Bread – primarily chapatis, rotis, naan and parathas – and poppadums are served at every meal, the slim folds of the freshly baked dough being perfect for transporting the delicious curries and barbecued meats from plate to mouth, and for wiping up sauce. Wheat is one of the most important crops in Pakistan, so it is not surprising that bread is such a staple, and although many people living in cities now buy their daily bread,

HOW TO PULP PAPAYA

Unripe papaya contains the enzyme papain, which acts as a tenderizing agent on meat. It is very simple to use: simply remove the skin and seeds from a green papaya and chop the flesh into cubes. Transfer the pieces to a blender or food processor and blitz to form a pulp. Combine the pulp with whichever spices are suggested in the recipe, and leave the meat to marinate. Any unused pulp can be frozen for future use.

HOW TO MAKE CHAPATIS

makes 16

400g/14oz/3½ cups chapati flour (atta) or fine wholemeal (whole-wheat) flour, plus a little extra for dusting
5ml/1 tsp salt
250ml/9fl oz/1 cup water

1 Combine the flour and salt in a bowl. Gradually add the water. Continue to mix until a dough is formed.

2 Transfer the dough to a lightly floured surface and knead it for 4–5 minutes. When all the excess moisture has been absorbed by the flour, wrap the dough in clear film (plastic wrap) and let it rest for 30 minutes. Alternatively, make the dough in a food processor, following the manufacturer's instructions.

3 Divide the dough into two equal parts and pinch or cut eight equal portions from each. Form the portions into balls and flatten them into neat, round cakes. Dust lightly in the flour and roll each one out to a 15cm/6in circle. Keep the rest covered with a damp dish towel while you work.

4 Preheat a heavy cast-iron griddle over a medium/high heat. Place a dough circle on it, cook for about 30 seconds, then turn it over using a metal spatula. Cook until bubbles begin to appear on the surface and turn it over again. Press the edges down gently with a clean dish towel to encourage the chapati to puff up (they will not always puff up, but this does not affect the taste).

5 Cook until the underneath begins to brown, then remove from the heat and keep them hot by wrapping them in foil lined with kitchen paper while you cook the remaining breads.

ABOVE, LEFT TO RIGHT Chickpeas and lentils are very important sources of nutrition in Pakistan.

others prefer to make it themselves at home, so it can be enjoyed fresh from the hotplate.

Rice (preferably basmati) is often served alongside the ubiquitous bread, usually simply boiled (chawal) and served with daal, but sometimes mixed with cooked chickpeas, chopped vegetables or some lentils (kichdi). It is also elevated to celebratory status in the many renowned pulaos and biryanis that are such a feature of weddings and other special occasions, where it is a symbol of wealth and success.

Lentils are a very important food source in Pakistan, bringing protein, fibre and many different nutrients to the table of even the poorest person. Extremely versatile, they can be cooked to a smooth paste, used to make soup and added to other dishes to bulk them out and give flavour and texture. The most common types in Pakistan are chana daal (split Bengal gram), masoor daal (red split lentils) and toor daal (pigeon peas). Chickpeas, or chana, are another dominant feature on the Pakistani culinary landscape, appearing in the much-loved breakfast dish cholay, a huge range of chaats or little snacks, in various rice dishes and alongside meat or poultry in curries. Their nutty flavour and firm or smooth texture (depending upon the type) are the perfect foil to spices, and they are also very nutritious.

KEY TECHNIQUES

Pakistani cooking is generally fairly straightforward, but to produce top-quality, authentic results it is best to use the tried-and-tested techniques outlined below and in the recipes.

THE SECRET OF A GOOD CURRY The final colour and texture of a curry depends on how well you browned the onions in the first stage. This requires patience, especially if you are cooking a large quantity. Heat the oil first, before you add the onions, then reduce the heat slightly so that the onions go golden brown without burning, and stir them gently and frequently with a wooden spoon or spatula.

Once this is done, add the spices, meat or other ingredients, and mix and coat the meat by frying and stirring in semi-circular movements, scraping the bottom of the pan (bhoona). This is essential for a good end result.

HOW TO COOK BASMATI RICE

serves 4

275g/10oz/1⅓ cups basmati rice
15ml/1 tbsp butter
2.5ml/½ tsp salt

1 Put the rice in a strainer and rinse it under cold running water for at least 1 minute, until the water runs clear. Transfer it to a bowl and soak it in fresh water for 20–30 minutes. Drain well.
2 In a medium-sized pan, bring 550ml/18fl oz/2½ cups water to the boil and add the butter, salt and the drained rice. Bring it to the boil and let it simmer steadily for 1 minute.
3 Reduce the heat to low and cover the pan tightly. Cook for 8–9 minutes, then switch off the heat source. Leave the pan to stand undisturbed with its lid on for 10–12 minutes.
4 Fluff up the rice with a fork or slotted spoon and serve with a main course or vegetable side dishes.

USING SPICES There are many ways of cooking with spices. You can use them whole, ground, roasted, fried or mixed with yogurt to marinate meat and poultry. One spice can completely alter the flavour of a dish and a combination of several can produce very different colours and textures.

The quantities of spices given in the recipes are merely a guide. Do not hesitate to increase or decrease these as you wish, especially in the cases of salt and chilli powder, which are very much a

MAKING A BAGHAAR (SEASONED OIL DRESSING)

A baghaar is a classic way to finish some Pakistani dishes, and really boosts the flavour. To make one, oil or ghee is heated to a very high temperature, without burning. The spices, onions and herbs are dropped into the sizzling oil, immediately changing colour and becoming very aromatic. The seasoned oil is then removed from the heat and poured over the dish – cooked daals or vegetables – often like a dressing. Sometimes uncooked food is added to the heated oil, to be simmered or sautéed. You will find full instructions for baghaars in the recipes.

matter of personal taste. Remember that prolonged cooking over a low heat will always improve the taste of the food as it allows the spices to be properly absorbed. This is why reheating the following day should not be a problem in the case of most Pakistani food. Do feel free to experiment with the different spices and, above all, taste everything.

Many of the recipes in this book require ground spices, which are generally available in supermarkets as well as in Pakistani and Asian grocery stores. In Pakistan, we almost always buy whole spices and grind them ourselves. There is no doubt that freshly ground spices do make a noticeable difference to the taste, so do this if you have the time. However, there is no denying that it is more convenient, and quicker, to use ready-ground spices.

For some of the recipes, the spices need to be roasted. In Pakistan this is normally done on a tawa, but you can use a heavy, ideally cast-iron, frying pan instead. No water or oil is added to the spices – they are simply dry-roasted whole while the pan is shaken to stop them burning. If they are to be ground, do this after roasting.

PRESENTATION There are few 'rules' about presenting Pakistani food, but if you are entertaining have in mind which containers you will use for each dish and try not to neglect the final decorative touches – the fresh coriander or cilantro leaves, or the chopped chilli – that make the food look as appetizing as it tastes.

In Pakistan, curries and daals are served in large, deep dishes, rice is piled on flat, oval dishes and raita is served in a sauceboat or bowl. Breads should be served on a plate wrapped in foil to keep them warm and soft for as long as possible. Pickles, chutneys and kachoomer (onions and tomatoes in lemon juice) are eaten in small portions so it is best to put these in little bowls, each with a teaspoon, so that people do not take too much.

Guests usually help themselves from the serving dishes. Rice is placed in the centre of the dinner plate, leaving some room for the curries, which are never put on top of the rice. It is not necessary to pile everything from the table on to a dinner plate all at once.

Though you will probably wish to provide a cruet set at the table, it is a mistake to add salt before tasting a dish as it will have already been included with all the spices during cooking.

Decoration for the food, such as fresh coriander leaves and fresh green or red chilli, is best if fresh, but both of these items can be kept fairly well in the refrigerator in plastic bags or small freezer containers for convenience. Coriander is fairly easy to grow in the back garden, especially in the summer months, or on a sunny windowsill – so it is worth giving it a go if you use the herb regularly. Other garnishes, especially for kebabs or dry chicken pieces, include fine onion rings, tomatoes and lemon wedges, all of which are both attractive and inexpensive and add colour and flavour to the finished dish.

By contrast, a rather special way of decorating both savoury dishes and desserts is to use warq (beaten edible silver leaf). This method of decoration probably started with the Moghuls, perhaps seeking to intrigue their guests at palace banquets, and is reserved for very special occasions because it is quite an expensive item. A dessert decorated with warq certainly looks very beautiful, and is bound to impress your guests, becoming a talking point. However, it is real silver, so it may not be very pleasant for anyone with fillings in their teeth.

BELOW A little effort and a few attractive garnishes make all the difference to food presentation.

SNACKS & STREET FOOD

RECIPES

SERVES 4

2 large potatoes
400g/14oz canned chickpeas
7.5ml/1½ tsp salt
5ml/1 tsp chilli powder
15ml/1 tbsp lemon juice
30ml/2 tbsp chopped fresh
 coriander (cilantro)
10ml/2 tsp chaat masala
30ml/2 tbsp tamarind sauce
1 fresh green chilli, chopped (optional)

ALOO CHAAT
POTATO AND CHICKPEA CHAAT

Chaat is the generic term for a snack or an appetizer, although since they can be quite filling, you could serve several different types together to constitute a full meal. They are often available along the roadside from little cabins or restaurants, served by the ladleful from steaming aromatic vats. They are usually sweet and sour and contain tamarind sauce. This recipe is just one of many types of aloo chaats, and is made using partially mashed potatoes and chickpeas. Do try it on a Sunday afternoon with tea or lassis.

1 Peel and dice the potatoes, then cook them in a large pan of boiling water for 10–15 minutes, until soft. Drain well, then return to the pan and roughly mash.

2 Drain the can of chickpeas and mix them into the potatoes. Add the salt, chilli powder and lemon juice, then taste and adjust the seasoning according to your personal preference.

3 Stir in half of the fresh coriander. Sprinkle the chaat masala on top and finally pour over the tamarind sauce.

4 Transfer to a serving dish and garnish with the remaining fresh coriander and the chopped chilli. Serve at room temperature.

COOK'S TIP

Good-quality chaat masala and tamarind sauce are now widely available in most Asian stores.

ALOO PAAPRI CHAAT
POTATOES WITH CHICKPEAS AND PAAPRI

This mouthwatering snack has a crunchy texture because of the paapri and sev and, like most chaats, it is eaten all over the country, especially in Punjab and Karachi and during Ramadan. To give it a sweet and savoury taste I use two different types of sauces, one being tamarind. Sev, which is made of gram flour, is almost always bought rather than being made at home. Paapri are very similar to poori and can also be purchased. However, if you wish to make them yourself, follow the recipe for gol gappay (see page 32) and crush them, which will give the same texture.

SERVES 4

- 2 large potatoes
- 400g/14oz canned chickpeas, drained
- 120–150ml/4fl oz–¼ pint/½–⅔ cup whole natural (plain) yogurt
- 5ml/1 tsp salt
- 7.5ml/1½ tsp chilli powder
- 10ml/2 tsp sugar
- 30–45ml/2–3 tbsp chaat masala
- 30–45ml/2–3 tbsp tamarind sauce
- 30ml/2 tbsp masala chilli sauce
- 6–8 paapri, crushed
- 45–60ml/3–4 tbsp sev
- 30ml/2 tbsp fresh pomegranate seeds
- 2.5ml/½ tsp ground coriander
- 2.5ml/½ tsp chilli powder
- 2 fresh green chillies, chopped
- 15ml/1 tbsp chopped fresh coriander (cilantro)

1 Peel and dice the potatoes, then cook them in a large pan of boiling water for 10–15 minutes, until soft. Drain and transfer to a large serving bowl, along with the drained canned chickpeas.

2 In a separate bowl, blend together the yogurt, salt, chilli powder, sugar and half the chaat masala. Now pour this yogurt mixture over the top of the potatoes and chickpeas and gently stir to combine. Wipe the sides of the dish clean.

3 To assemble, drizzle the tamarind sauce and the masala chilli sauce over the top of the potato and yogurt mixture, then top with the crushed paapri, sev, pomegranate seeds, remaining chaat masala, ground coriander, chilli powder, chopped green chilli and chopped fresh coriander. Serve at room temperature.

SADHA KHATTA MEETA CHAAT
SIMPLE SWEET-AND-SOUR CHAAT

Similar to other aloo chaats, this quick-to-assemble version features a raw chutney made from fresh herbs and some spices. Chutneys are popular everywhere in Pakistan, made in most households to family recipes that have been handed down from generation to generation. This chutney can also be served as an accompaniment to many curries along with poppadums, rice and bread in the traditional serving style, or with appetizers at modern wedding feasts.

1 Peel and finely dice the potatoes, then cook them in a large pan of boiling water for 10–15 minutes, until soft. Drain and leave to cool.

2 Meanwhile, make the chutney by blending together all the ingredients in a blender or food processor until they are smooth. Add a drop of water if necessary to thin down the mixture to a spooning consistency.

3 Put the cooled potatoes, diced onion, drained canned chickpeas and salt in a serving bowl and stir to combine.

4 Pour over the chutney and stir to combine. Wipe the sides of the dish clean so it looks neat. Garnish with fresh coriander and mint leaves and sprinkle with sév, then serve at room temperature.

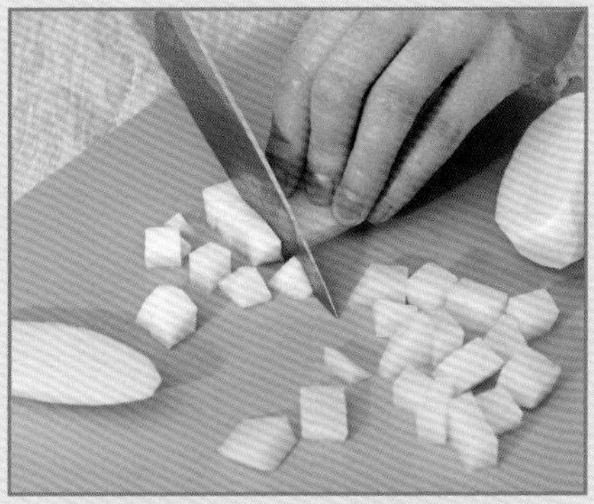

SERVES 4

2 medium potatoes
1 medium onion, peeled and finely diced
400g/14oz canned chickpeas, drained
5ml/1 tsp salt, or to taste
fresh coriander (cilantro) and mint leaves, to garnish
30–45ml/2–3 tbsp sev, for sprinkling

FOR THE CHUTNEY

6–8 fresh mint leaves
45ml/3 tbsp chopped fresh coriander (cilantro)
2 fresh green chillies, seeded and finely chopped
5ml/1 tsp ground cumin
5ml/1 tsp ground coriander
2.5ml/½ tsp ground ginger
5ml/1 tsp soft light brown sugar
15ml/1 tbsp lemon juice

COOK'S TIP

Sev consists of small pieces of crunchy deep-fried noodles made from gram flour. It lends texture and substance to this chaat, and is readily available in most Asian stores.

SERVES 4

2 small potatoes, peeled and diced
400g/14oz canned chickpeas, drained
1 medium onion, peeled and finely diced
5ml/1 tsp chilli powder
10ml/2 tsp sugar
2.5ml/½ tsp salt, or to taste
90–120ml/6–8 tbsp tamarind sauce
30ml/2 tbsp chaat masala
1 tomato, diced
15ml/1 tbsp lemon juice

TO GARNISH

1 large tomato, sliced
2 fresh green chillies (seeded if liked)
15ml/1 tbsp chopped fresh coriander (cilantro)
1 lemon, sliced and pips removed

CHOLAY

CHICKPEAS IN A SWEET-AND-SOUR SAUCE

Possibly one of the nation's most popular snacks, cholay is eaten all over Pakistan and is a must for iftar throughout the holy month of Ramadan. It also makes a delicious teatime treat any day.

1 Peel and finely dice the potatoes, then cook them in a large pan of boiling water for 10–15 minutes, until soft. Drain and leave to cool.

2 Put the chickpeas in a serving bowl, then add the cooled potatoes, onion, chilli powder, sugar, salt, tamarind sauce, half the chaat masala, tomato and lemon juice. Stir gently to combine.

3 Wipe the sides of the dish clean so it looks neat. Garnish with the sliced tomato, green chillies, fresh coriander, lemon slices and remaining chaat masala and serve at room temperature.

SERVES 4

- 60–75ml/4–5 tbsp vegetable oil
- 2 medium onions, peeled and finely chopped
- 5ml/1 tsp ginger pulp
- 5ml/1 tsp garlic pulp
- 5ml/1 tsp chilli powder
- 5ml/1 tsp ground coriander
- 5ml/1 tsp salt
- 400g/14oz canned chickpeas, drained
- 120ml/4fl oz/½ cup water
- 2.5ml/½ tsp garam masala
- 15ml/1 tbsp tamarind sauce (optional)
- pooris, to serve

CHANA MASALA
SPICED CHICKPEAS

Chana masala is served as part of a very traditional breakfast consisting of aloo ki bhujna – a semi-dry potato dish – semolina halwa, which is dry and sweet, and some freshly made pooris. The weekend starts on Friday in Pakistan, and the whole breakfast can often be bought from the local halwai and any roadside café, where this dish is fried up in very large kadahis. I add a little tamarind sauce to give it a tangy flavour, although this is not really authentic.

1 Heat the oil in a pan, add the finely chopped onion and stir-fry for 3–5 minutes, until beginning to soften.

2 Add the ginger, garlic, chilli powder, ground coriander, salt and chickpeas. Stir-fry over a medium-high heat for about 1 minute.

3 Add the water, cover the pan with a tight lid and cook for 5–7 minutes, until the onion is cooked and the chickpeas are hot.

4 Sprinkle over the garam masala and stir it in, together with the tamarind sauce, if using. Transfer to a serving dish and serve with pooris.

MAVAY KA CHAAT
SPICED FRUIT SALAD

This sweet-and-sour fruit cocktail is a must all over Pakistan in the holy month of Ramadan when, once the sun goes down, the fast is broken with a date, followed by a number of snacks. This chaat is also good at any other time of the year, using whichever fruits are in season, and forms part of the teas that are so popular with Pakistani ladies.

1 Place all of the prepared fruits and the orange segments, together with the syrup from the can, in a large serving bowl.

2 Sprinkle over the lemon juice, sugar, chaat masala, salt and pomegranate seeds and stir gently, trying not to break the fruit pieces. Serve immediately, garnished with mint.

VARIATION Drained canned guavas can also be used if fresh are not available. The drained syrup can be used in drinks or in place of the orange syrup.

SERVES 4

1 large apple, diced
10–15 white grapes, halved
2 fresh guavas, peeled and diced
3 bananas, peeled and chopped
1 small can (about 250g/9oz) orange segments in syrup
10ml/2 tsp lemon juice
10ml/2 tsp sugar
10–15ml/2–3 tsp chaat masala
2.5ml/½ tsp salt
45ml/3 tbsp pomegranate seeds
fresh mint, to garnish

MASALA ALOO CHIPS
SPICY POTATO FRIES

These mouthwatering fries are delicious for a snack at teatime and they are easy to cook at home, although they are sometimes sold on the street in major cities in Pakistan. They can be served with either a sweet-and-sour sauce or tamarind sauce. I've used chaat masala to flavour the fries, and pepped them up with a little crushed red chilli.

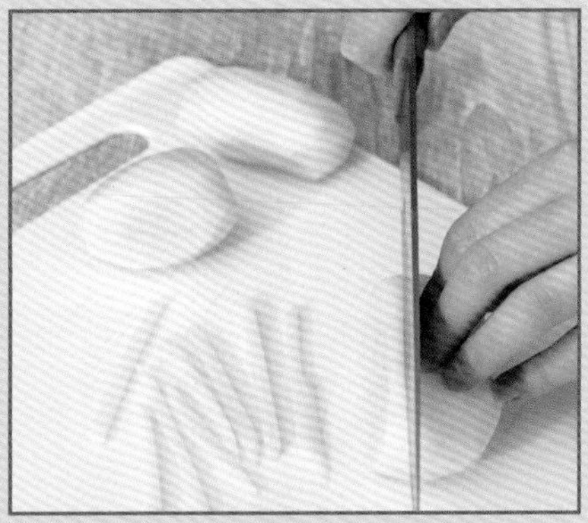

1 Peel the potatoes, then slice them into thin fries.

2 Blend together the salt, crushed red chilli, chaat masala and gram flour in a large bowl. Add the sliced potatoes and stir gently to completely coat the fries in the dry mixture.

3 Heat the oil in a wok, deep frying pan or deep-fat fryer to 190°C/375°F. It should come two-thirds of the way up whichever pan you use.

4 Very carefully lower the first batch of fries into the hot oil and cook until they are golden and crisp. The time taken will depend on the thickness of the fries, so stand over the pan and keep an eye on them.

5 Once cooked, carefully scoop out the fries using a wire basket or slotted spoon and drain them on kitchen paper. Repeat until all of the fries are cooked.

6 Serve immediately with a sauce of your choice.

SERVES 4

3 medium potatoes
5ml/1 tsp salt
5ml/1 tsp crushed red chilli
10ml/2 tsp chaat masala
15ml/1 tbsp gram flour
vegetable oil, for deep-frying
condiments, such as tomato sauce, masala sauce or chutney

COOK'S TIP

If you don't have a thermometer, you can test whether the oil is up to temperature by dropping in a cube of bread. If it browns in 1 minute, the oil is hot enough for deep-frying.

SERVES 4

3 large potatoes
50ml/2fl oz/¼ cup vegetable oil
1.5ml/¼ tsp onion seeds
4–6 curry leaves
5ml/1 tsp ginger pulp
5ml/1 tsp garlic pulp
7.5ml/1½ tsp chilli powder
2.5ml/½ tsp ground turmeric
5ml/1 tsp salt
2 fresh green chillies, chopped
15ml/1 tbsp chopped fresh coriander (cilantro)
50ml/2fl oz/¼ cup water
15ml/1 tbsp lemon juice
poori or chapatis, to serve

ALOO KI BHUJIA
SPICY STIR-FRIED POTATOES

This very simple potato dish forms part of a brunch that includes sooji halwa (caramelized sweet semolina paste) and chana masala. It also makes a great accompaniment to any dish, or it can be eaten on its own with a poori and a dollop of mango chutney.

1 Peel and roughly dice the potatoes.

2 Heat the oil in a wok or heavy frying pan over a medium heat, then add the onion seeds and curry leaves and stir-fry for about 1 minute.

3 Add the potatoes, followed by the ginger, garlic, chilli powder, ground turmeric and salt. Stir-fry for about 10 minutes.

4 Add half the chopped green chillies and half the fresh coriander, followed by the water. Cover the pan with a lid, lower the heat and cook for 10–15 minutes. Check the potatoes; they should be quite soft, but not mushy.

5 Stir, then add the remaining green chillies and fresh coriander followed by the lemon juice. Serve with poori or chapatis.

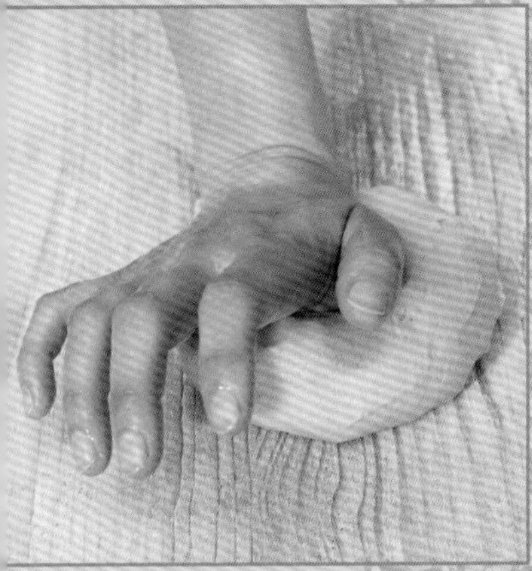

GOL GAPPAY
POORIS WITH CHICKPEAS AND GINGER SAUCE

An extremely popular street food, this snack is also known as pani poori. The little round pooris are tiny enough that you can easily eat four or five at a time, and are served with a ginger-flavoured water along with some chickpeas and different sauces, such as date chutney and tamarind sauce. You can either present the various components separately and allow diners to assemble their own gol gappay, or you can make them up and present them ready-plated. If you choose the latter option, ensure you serve them straight away as they quickly go soggy, especially when made with ginger water.

SERVES 4

400g/14oz canned chickpeas, drained
Date and Tamarind Chutney (see page 182)

FOR THE POORIS
175g/6oz/1½ cups brown atta flour
1.5ml/¼ tsp bicarbonate of soda (baking soda)
15ml/1 tbsp coarse semolina
2.5ml/½ tsp salt
120–175ml/4–6fl oz/½–¾ cup water
vegetable oil, for deep-frying

FOR THE SPICY GINGER SAUCE (SAUNT)
750ml/1¼ pints/3 cups water
5ml/1 tsp ground ginger
2.5ml/½ tsp chilli powder
5ml/1 tsp ground cumin
2.5ml/½ tsp salt
15ml/1 tbsp tamarind sauce
10ml/2 tsp powdered jaggery
5ml/1 tsp finely chopped fresh coriander (cilantro)

1 First make the pooris. Put the atta flour in a large bowl, then add the bicarbonate of soda, semolina and salt and mix everything thoroughly.

2 Make a well in the middle of the dry ingredients, then gradually pour in enough water to make a fairly stiff dough. It is best to do this with your hands.

3 Turn out the dough on to a lightly oiled surface and knead with oiled hands for about 20 minutes. The dough should be stiff and tight. Cover with a damp cloth and leave to rest for about 1 hour.

4 Meanwhile, make the spicy ginger sauce. Bring the water to the boil in a pan, lower the heat and add all of the sauce ingredients. Simmer for about 5 minutes, then pour into a jug or pitcher and set aside.

5 Oil your hands, then knead the dough for a further 20–25 minutes. Break off about 12 small balls of dough and roll these out to rounds about 5cm/2in in diameter. Cover the rolled with a dish towel while you roll out the remaining balls.

6 Two-thirds fill a large wok or kadahi with oil and place over a medium-high heat, until steaming. Reduce the heat to medium-low. Carefully lower one poori at a time into the hot oil with a slotted spoon. Continuously spoon oil over the top of the poori as it cooks, to achieve even cooking and so that it puffs up.

7 Transfer the cooked pooris to a plate lined with kitchen paper and cook the remaining dough discs in the same way. Once drained of oil, transfer the cooked pooris to a large serving platter.

8 Assemble the gol gappays by gently piercing a small hole in the middle of the pooris and pouring a few chickpeas into the hollow cavity, followed by the date and tamarind chutney and the spicy ginger sauce. Serve immediately.

VARIATION You could also use any green chilli chutney or a masala tomato sauce, if you prefer.

COOK'S TIPS

- These pooris can also be broken roughly and used on top of a chana chaat, to add a crispy texture.
- As pooris are time-consuming to make, you may prefer to buy ready-made ones from an Asian supermarket.

KARACHI-STYLE BUN KEBABS
POTATO AND LENTIL PATTIES

Served in a soft burger bun, these vegetarian kebabs are comprised of potatoes and chana daal and make a delicious alternative to classic beef burgers. They are commonly eaten on the bustling streets of Karachi, served with mint or tamarind chutney along with other garnishes, such as sliced onions and tomatoes.

SERVES 4–6

2 large potatoes
225g/8oz/1 cup chana daal, rinsed and soaked in water for 1 hour
7.5ml/1½ tsp ground cumin
12.5ml/2½ tsp ground coriander
10ml/2 tsp crushed dried red chillies, or to taste
7.5ml/1½ tsp salt, or to taste
4–6 fresh mint leaves, finely chopped
12.5ml/2½ tsp mango powder (alamchoor)
30ml/2 tbsp chaat masala
2 eggs
vegetable oil, for shallow-frying
4–6 burger buns, split in half

TO SERVE

2 tomatoes, sliced
1 onion, peeled and sliced into rings
Mint and Raw Mango Chutney (see page 183)

1 Peel and dice the potatoes, then cook them in a large pan of boiling water for 10–15 minutes, until soft. Drain well, then return to the pan and mash until smooth. Transfer to a large bowl and leave to cool.

2 Meanwhile, drain the chana daal, then cook it in a large pan of boiling water for 20–30 minutes, until soft. Drain and mash until it forms a paste.

3 Add the chana daal paste to the bowl of mashed potato, followed by the ground cumin, ground coriander, crushed dried red chillies, salt, mint leaves, mango powder and chaat masala. Mix really well to combine, then taste and adjust the seasoning as necessary.

4 Whisk the eggs in a small, shallow dish.

5 Grease your hands with a little oil and break off 4–6 balls of the potato mixture, each a little larger than a golf ball. Form these into patties with your hands.

6 Dip each patty into the whisked egg. There may be some egg left over, which can be fried and sliced after you have cooked the patties to make a pleasant addition to each bun.

7 Heat the oil in a large frying pan over a low heat, then add the patties. Fry for 3–4 minutes, then carefully flip them over and fry on the other side for 3–4 minutes, until both sides are golden brown. Take care not to break up the patties.

8 Meanwhile, heat a little oil in a separate pan and lightly fry both sides of each of the burger buns, until golden brown.

9 Place a fried patty on one half of a burger bun, top with a little of the fried egg if there is any, some sliced tomato, onion rings and a little mint and raw mango chutney, then top with the other half of the burger bun. Repeat for all the buns.

BHUNA BHUTTA
BARBECUED CORN ON THE COB

Spicy roasted corn on the cob is probably one of the oldest and most popular street foods in Pakistan. Normally it is barbecued on live coal flames at roadside stalls and rotated until it is roasted entirely, meaning it is ideal for cooking on the barbecue, but it is equally easy to achieve the same result (albeit without such a smoky flavour) under a hot grill or broiler.

1 Preheat a grill or broiler to high, or prepare a barbecue; it is ready for cooking once the coals are grey and covered in a fine layer of ash.

2 Pull off the outer layers of the husk from the corn on the cob, leaving the layers still connected as the cooked corn is served in its own skin. Just remove the silky strands and fold back the husks.

3 Place the corn on a grill pan or on the bars of the barbecue and cook for 12–15 minutes, turning every 4–5 minutes, until the corn is golden brown all over.

4 Remove the corn from the heat and brush each one with melted butter, squeeze over a little lemon juice, and sprinkle with salt, chilli powder and chaat masala. Serve in its own skin on a plate.

SERVES 4

4 fresh corn on the cob
60ml/4 tbsp butter, melted
30ml/2 tbsp lemon juice
10ml/2 tsp salt
2.5–5ml/½–1 tsp chilli powder
30–45ml/2–3 tbsp chaat masala

VARIATION

This recipe is best made with fresh corn on the cob when it is in season, but you could use thawed frozen cobs at other times of the year.

SERVES 4

12 small chicken wings
5ml/1 tsp salt
15ml/1 tbsp lemon juice
5ml/1 tsp crushed dried red chillies
60–75ml/4–5 tbsp vegetable oil
1.5ml/¼ tsp onion seeds
4–6 curry leaves
5ml/1 tsp ginger pulp
5ml/1 tsp sugar
7.5ml/1½ tsp chilli powder
2.5ml/½ tsp ground turmeric
30ml/2 tbsp mango chutney
120ml/4fl oz/½ cup water
1 bunch spring onions (scallions), roughly chopped
1 large green (bell) pepper, seeded and sliced
1 lemon, sliced, to serve

KHATTAY MEETAY MURGH KAY KEBABS

SWEET-AND-SOUR CHICKEN WINGS

Chinese food has been a great favourite in Pakistan for many years, especially in Karachi, where fabulous Chinese restaurants have been in vogue since at least the early 1970s. This trend is due in small part to Pakistan's proximity to China, but more because Pakistanis love the cuisine and globalization has made it ubiquitous. In this dish, the sweet-and-sour flavour is a nod to this Chinese influence – a modern twist on an old Pakistani classic.

1 Rub the chicken wings all over with the salt, lemon juice and crushed dried red chillies, then place in a dish, cover and marinate for a few hours in the refrigerator.

2 When you are ready to cook, heat the oil in a large wok or other heavy pan over a medium heat, then add the onion seeds and curry leaves and stir-fry for 1 minute.

3 Add the marinated chicken wings to the pan and stir-fry for 3–4 minutes, until sealed all over, then add the ginger pulp, sugar, chilli powder, ground turmeric and mango chutney. Stir to blend everything together, then add the water and stir once more, to combine.

4 Cover and cook for 10–15 minutes, stirring occasionally, or until the chicken wings are cooked and the water has evaporated.

5 Stir in the chopped spring onions and sliced green pepper and transfer to a serving dish. Serve piping hot with lemon slices for squeezing over.

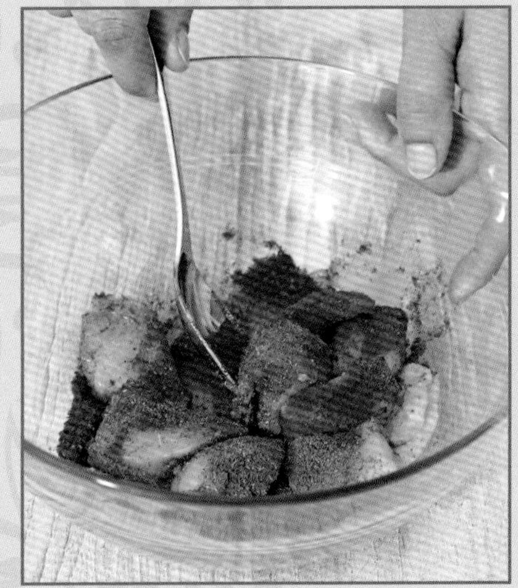

MURGH KAY PAKORAY
CHICKEN PAKORAS

Pakoras are little deep-fried morsels made using a gram-flour batter. The most popular type are onion pakoras, but potatoes, aubergines (eggplants) and fresh chillies can all be dipped and fried in the same manner. For this version, cubes of tender marinated chicken are slicked in a lightly spiced batter, creating a mouthwatering snack. The fried cubes can also be presented as an appetizer with some salad and lemon wedges.

SERVES 4

1 large skinless chicken breast fillet, cubed
5ml/1 tsp ginger pulp
5ml/1 tsp garlic pulp
7.5ml/1½ tsp chilli powder
5ml/1 tsp salt
10ml/2 tsp chaat masala
spicy tomato sauce and/or salad and lemon wedges, to serve

FOR THE BATTER

175g/6oz/1½ cups gram flour
7.5ml/1½ tsp crushed dried red chillies
2.5ml/½ tsp white cumin seeds
2 fresh green chillies, finely chopped
30ml/2 tbsp finely chopped fresh coriander (cilantro)
2.5ml/½ tsp baking powder
5ml/1 tsp salt
15ml/1 tbsp whole natural (plain) yogurt
about 250ml/8fl oz/1 cup water
vegetable oil, for deep-frying

1 Put the chicken cubes in a large bowl along with the ginger, garlic, chilli powder, salt and chaat masala. Mix together well, cover and set aside to marinate while you make the batter.

2 Sift the gram flour into a mixing bowl, then add the crushed dried red chillies, cumin seeds, fresh chillies, fresh coriander, baking powder and salt.

3 Stir well to combine, then make a well in the centre and add the yogurt and enough water to create a batter that is smooth but not too thick; it should be just thick enough to coat the chicken pieces.

4 Two-thirds fill a wok or deep, heavy pan with oil and place over a medium-high heat. Once the oil is shimmering, reduce the temperature to medium.

5 Dip a few cubes of the marinated chicken into the batter, drain off any excess and carefully lower into the hot oil on a slotted spoon. Fry for 3–4 minutes, until they are thoroughly cooked and golden brown.

6 Transfer to a plate lined with kitchen paper and repeat the process until all of the chicken is cooked. Serve immediately with spicy tomato sauce and/or some salad and lemon wedges.

SEAFOOD & FISH

RECIPES

BADAY JHINGAY PYAAZ AUR SIMLA MIRCH
TIGER PRAWNS WITH SHALLOTS AND PEPPERS

SEEKHDHAR LASSUN KAY BADAY JHINGAY
GRILLED GARLIC KING PRAWNS

SOOKHAY MASALA JHINGAY
CRISPY SPICY PRAWNS

TANDOORI JHINGAY
TANDOORI-STYLE PRAWNS

LAHORI THALI HUWI MACHLI
LAHORI FRIED FISH

MIRCH VALI MACHLI
CHILLI-FRIED COD

BADAY JHINGAY PYAAZ AUR SIMLA MIRCH

TIGER PRAWNS WITH SHALLOTS AND PEPPERS

Sold in vast quantities from simple plastic boxes at the many daily markets that take place nationwide, prawns are without a doubt the most popular form of seafood consumed in Pakistan. Here, the use of fennel seeds along with crushed red chillies provide a distinctive flavour and aroma, while the crunchy squares of raw bell pepper provide a foil to the tender prawns. It is best cooked in a kadahi, a wok-like utensil used mostly in the northernmost provinces of Pakistan, but a wok can also be used.

SERVES 4

- 90–120ml/6–8 tbsp vegetable oil
- 2.5ml/½ tsp fennel seeds
- 2.5ml/½ tsp onion seeds
- 7.5ml/1½ tsp crushed dried red chillies
- 5ml/1 tsp garlic pulp
- 12 shallots, peeled
- 2.5ml/½ tsp salt, or to taste
- 12–16 cooked tiger prawns (shrimp)
- 1 red (bell) pepper, seeded and cut into large squares
- 30ml/2 tbsp chopped fresh coriander (cilantro)
- 30ml/2 tbsp lemon juice

1 Heat the oil in a wok or frying pan over a medium heat. Add the fennel seeds, onion seeds, crushed dried red chillies, garlic and shallots and fry over a low-medium heat for about 10 minutes, stirring frequently, until the shallots are golden brown.

2 Add the salt and prawns and stir-fry for 3–5 minutes, until the prawns are hot.

3 Stir in the red pepper and fresh coriander and serve immediately, sprinkled with the lemon juice.

SERVES 4

12 raw king prawns (jumbo shrimp)
5ml/1 tsp tomato paste
5ml/1 tsp garlic pulp
5ml/1 tsp ground coriander
5ml/1 tsp ground cumin
7.5ml/1½ tsp chilli powder
5ml/1 tsp paprika
5ml/1 tsp salt
30ml/2 tbsp chopped fresh coriander (cilantro)
45ml/3 tbsp lemon juice
lemon slices and salad leaves, to garnish

SEEKHDHAR LASSUN KAY BADAY JHINGAY

GRILLED GARLIC KING PRAWNS

Large prawns are an important food source in Pakistan, where they are found in the many mangrove swamps as well as an increasing number of freshwater prawn farms. Choose good-quality large ones as they tend to shrink a little under the grill. This simple dish can be served as an appetizer or as a part of a mixed grill platter.

1 Put the prawns in a bowl, then add the tomato paste, garlic, ground coriander, ground cumin, chilli powder, paprika, salt, half of the fresh coriander and the lemon juice.

2 Stir to combine thoroughly, then cover and leave to marinate for about 1 hour in the refrigerator.

3 Preheat the grill or broiler and place the prawns on a baking sheet. Grill them, turning them at least once, for 7–10 minutes, keeping a close eye on them so that they do not brown.

4 Remove and transfer to a serving plate. Garnish with lemon slices and some salad leaves, and serve.

SOOKHAY MASALA JHINGAY
CRISPY SPICY PRAWNS

These spicy deep-fried marinated prawns are delicious either as a snack or as an appetizer, served with chilli sauce and a side salad. Simple to make at home, this dish is also a feature of the lavish high-tea spreads found at all good hotels in Pakistan.

SERVES 4

8–12 raw king prawns (jumbo shrimp)
5ml/1 tsp ginger pulp
7.5ml/1½ tsp crushed dried red chillies
2.5ml/½ tsp salt
30ml/2 tbsp hot chilli sauce
30ml/2 tbsp very finely chopped fresh coriander (cilantro)
vegetable oil, for deep-frying
chilli and garlic sauce or a chutney of your choice, to serve
lemon wedges, to garnish

FOR THE COATING

60ml/4 tbsp cornflour (cornstarch)
2.5ml/½ tsp salt
2.5ml/½ tsp ground white pepper
1 egg white
120ml/4fl oz/½ cup milk

1 In a bowl, mix together the prawns, ginger, crushed dried red chillies, salt, hot chilli sauce and chopped fresh coriander. Cover and set aside to marinate in the refrigerator for about 30 minutes.

2 Meanwhile, make the batter. Mix together the cornflour, salt and pepper in one bowl. In a separate bowl, whisk together the egg white and milk.

3 Two-thirds fill a wok or deep, heavy pan with oil, then place it over a medium-high heat, until it is shimmering.

4 Working quickly with one prawn at a time, dip a prawn first into the cornflour mixture, then into the egg and milk mixture, then into the cornflour mixture again. Carefully place the coated prawn in the hot oil and repeat the process with two or three more prawns. Do not overcrowd the pan.

5 Deep-fry the prawns for 4–5 minutes, until golden brown, then lift out with a slotted spoon and drain on kitchen paper. Repeat the dipping and cooking process with the remaining prawns.

6 Serve the prawns immediately with a sauce or chutney of your choice, garnished with lemon wedges.

TANDOORI JHINGAY
TANDOORI-STYLE PRAWNS

This mouthwatering dish can be served as an appetizer arranged on a bed of lettuce with a lemon wedge, or as an attractive side dish for almost any meal. Though not essential, it is best to shell the prawns before cooking them as some people find it a bit awkward to shell them at the table.

SERVES 4

12 raw king or tiger prawns (jumbo shrimp)
115g/4oz/½ cup unsalted butter
30ml/2 tbsp vegetable oil
5ml/1 tsp garlic pulp
5ml/1 tsp ginger pulp
10ml/2 tsp chilli powder
5ml/1 tsp salt
10ml/2 tsp ground coriander
5ml/1 tsp ground cumin
15ml/1 tbsp finely chopped fresh coriander (cilantro)

TO GARNISH

8 lettuce leaves
1 small onion, peeled and cut into rings
1–2 fresh freen chillies, finely chopped
1 lemon, cut into wedges

1 First, prepare the prawns. Pull off the heads and remove the shells, then use the tip of a sharp knife to remove the thin black line that runs along the back of the prawn. Rinse the prawns and pat them dry. Place them on an ovenproof dish or pan that can go under the grill or broiler.

2 Melt the butter in a small pan over a low heat, then stir in the oil, garlic, ginger, chilli powder, salt, ground coriander, ground cumin and fresh coriander. Preheat a grill to high.

3 Brush the melted butter mixture on the prawns, then place them under the very hot grill and cook for 10–12 minutes, turning once, until cooked through.

4 Arrange a bed of lettuce leaves on a serving platter, then top with the cooked prawns, onion rings, finely chopped fresh chilli and lemon wedges. Serve immediately.

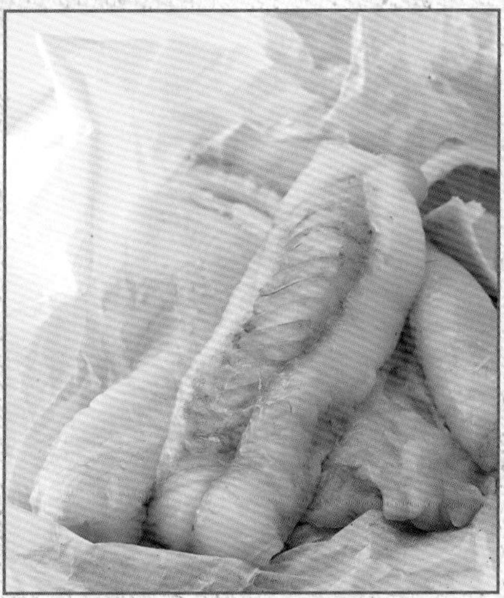

LAHORI THALI HUWI MACHLI

LAHORI FRIED FISH

Wonderfully crisp, this fish is delicious as an appetizer with a salad and some tamarind chutney, or it can be served as part of a main meal. Monkfish has a lovely meaty texture that stands up well to the spices as well as the deep-frying in this recipe, although in Pakistan the fish would more likely be pomfrey or rohu.

SERVES 4

1 monkfish, skinned, filleted and cut into 15 pieces about 5cm/2in in size (ask your fishmonger to do this for you, if you prefer)
60ml/4 tbsp lemon juice
5ml/1 tsp ginger pulp
5ml/1 tsp garlic pulp
7.5ml/1½ tsp salt
10–15ml/2–3 tsp chaat masala
10ml/2 tsp crushed dried red chillies
tamarind sauce or chilli sauce, to serve
lemon wedges, to garnish

FOR THE BATTER

60ml/4 tbsp gram flour
30ml/2 tbsp rice flour
1.5ml/¼ tsp baking powder
5ml/1 tsp salt
5ml/1 tsp garam masala
7.5ml/1½ tsp chilli powder
2.5ml/½ tsp ground turmeric
5ml/1 tsp crushed coriander seeds
5ml/1 tsp crushed cumin seeds
90ml/6 tbsp water
vegetable oil, for deep-frying

1 Put the monkfish cubes in a bowl with the lemon juice, ginger, garlic, salt, half of the chaat masala, and the crushed dried red chillies. Mix well, cover and leave to marinate in the refrigerator for about 30 minutes.

2 Meanwhile, make the batter. Sift the gram flour into a large bowl, then mix in the rice flour, baking powder, salt, garam masala, chilli powder, ground turmeric, and the crushed coriander and cumin seeds.

3 Make a well in the centre of the dry ingredients, then slowly pour in the water, gently whisking it as you mix everything to form a thick and smooth batter.

4 Two-thirds fill a deep wok or deep, heavy pan with oil, then place over a medium-high heat, until shimmering. Reduce the heat to medium.

5 Working methodically, dip a few pieces of the fish into the batter, allowing any excess to drain off, then carefully lower these into the hot oil. Do not overcrowd the pan.

6 Fry the fish for 4–5 minutes, until golden brown. Carefully remove to a plate lined with kitchen paper using a slotted spoon, and repeat the dipping and cooking process with the remaining fish.

7 When all the fish is cooked, serve it with tamarind sauce or any chilli sauce of your choice, garnished with lemon wedges.

MIRCH VALI MACHLI
CHILLI-FRIED COD

This fiery dish is not for the faint-hearted, but it is very popular among aficionados with a palate for hot and spicy food. It is wonderful as part of a main meal, served alongside some boiled rice and raita or any other curry. Pomfrey would be used in Pakistan, but any white fish works well – the more sustainable the better.

SERVES 4

15ml/1 tbsp crushed coriander seeds
15ml/1 tbsp cumin seeds
7.5ml/1½ tsp crushed dried red chillies
7.5ml/1½ tsp chaat masala
7.5ml/1½ tsp chilli powder
5ml/1 tsp ginger pulp
5ml/1 tsp garlic pulp
7.5ml/1½ tsp salt
30ml/2 tbsp masala chilli sauce
30ml/2 tbsp cornflour (cornstarch)
1 medium onion, peeled and finely chopped
2 medium fresh green chillies, finely chopped
30ml/2 tbsp chopped fresh coriander (cilantro)
1 large white fish fillet, skinned and cut into pieces about 5cm/2in in size
vegetable oil, for deep-frying
plain boiled rice and raita, to serve
lemon wedges and sprigs of fresh coriander, to garnish

1 Crush the coriander and cumin seeds together using a mortar and pestle.

2 Transfer the crushed spices to a large bowl, then add the crushed dried red chillies, chaat masala, chilli powder, ginger, garlic, salt, masala chilli sauce, cornflour, onion, fresh chilli and fresh coriander. Stir to combine thoroughly.

3 Gently stir in the fish pieces, then cover and leave to marinate in the refrigerator for about 2 hours.

4 Two-thirds fill a deep wok or deep, heavy pan with oil, then place over a medium-high heat, until shimmering. Reduce the heat to medium.

5 Carefully lower in a few pieces of the fish and fry for 2–3 minutes, until cooked through, then carefully transfer to a plate lined with kitchen paper with a slotted spoon, and fry the remaining fish in the same way.

6 Serve with plain boiled rice and raita, garnished with lemon wedges and some sprigs of fresh coriander.

CHICKEN

RECIPES

MURGH AUR SUBZEE KI YAKHNEE
CLEAR CHICKEN AND VEGETABLE CONSOMMÉ

TANDOORI MURGH
TANDOORI CHICKEN

ALOO AUR NIMBOO KI MURGH
POTATO AND LEMON CHICKEN

LAHORI MURGH KADAHI
LAHORI CHICKEN

MURGH DOPIAZA
CHICKEN DOPIAZA

KADAHI MURGH QEEMA
FRIED MINCED CHICKEN

PALAK MURGH
CHICKEN WITH SPINACH

HARA MASALA MURGH
CHICKEN WITH GREEN SPICES

MASALA MURGH
PAKISTANI FRIED CHICKEN

MASALA MALAIDHAAR MURGH
MASALA CREAMY CHICKEN

KASHMIRI MURGH
KASHMIRI CHICKEN WITH DRIED FRUITS

CHOLAY MURGH
CHICKEN WITH CHICKPEAS

LAHORI MURGH CHARGHA
LAHORI STEAMED CHICKEN

MALAI MURGH TIKKA
MALAI CHICKEN TIKKA

ACHARI MURGH
CHICKEN COOKED WITH PICKLING SPICES

KAT-A-KAT MURGH
KAT-A-KAT CHICKEN

MURGH AUR SUBZEE KI YAKHNEE

CLEAR CHICKEN AND VEGETABLE CONSOMMÉ

Prepare this nourishing Raj-derived broth for a cold winter's day, when it is especially delicious served with flat garlic bread or any toasted bread you like. As a child, my mother used to give this to me when I had a cold, and I still use the same recipe today if I feel under the weather.

SERVES 4

- 1 baby chicken, cut into 8 pieces
- 30ml/2 tbsp lemon juice
- 2.5ml/½ tsp ground nutmeg
- 5ml/1 tsp salt, or to taste
- 2.5ml/½ tsp coarse ground pepper
- 1 bay leaf
- 75–115g/3–4oz frozen carrot, green bean and pea mixture, thawed, or the equivalent weight of peeled and diced fresh carrots, chopped green beans and podded peas
- 900ml/1½ pints/3¾ cups water
- flat garlic bread or any toasted bread, to serve

1 Put the prepared chicken in a large pan. Add the lemon juice, ground nutmeg, salt, pepper, bay leaf, vegetables and water.

2 Stir to combine with a wooden spoon, then part-cover the pan with a lid, leaving the large spoon in place to keep the lid propped open and to prevent it from boiling over.

3 Simmer over a low heat for 35–40 minutes, by which time the liquid will have reduced a little.

4 Taste and adjust the seasoning to suit your taste, then drain the liquid through a strainer into a large bowl.

5 You can either serve the consommé on its own or you could add the flesh from the chicken and the vegetables to the clear soup. Serve hot with bread.

TANDOORI MURGH
TANDOORI CHICKEN

This famous dish gets its name from the blisteringly hot tandoor (clay oven) that is the dominant feature of the cuisine in the North-West Frontier Province. Today, tandoors are used more widely, although the cooking style is still the hallmark of the frontier region and visitors and inhabitants can choose from countless wonderful open-air restaurants that specialize only in tandoori dishes. It is unlikely that you will have one in your home, if you have an outdoor wood-fired oven this is perfect but otherwise you can replicate the high temperature (if not the aromatic smokiness and tantalizing sizzle) by setting a conventional oven to its highest temperature.

1 Divide the chicken into legs and breasts by removing the legs using a sharp knife, then removing the wings (use these for making stock or for another recipe). Locate and remove the wishbone, then carefully slice off the two breasts, starting by slicing along the breastbone and then working down using a smooth cutting action. Use the carcass for making stock. Alternatively, you can buy ready-prepared leg (not drumstick) and breast portions.

2 Remove the skin and then make deep cuts in the flesh to allow the marinade to permeate the chicken.

3 Pour the yogurt into a large bowl and add the garam masala, garlic, ginger, ground cumin, ground coriander, chilli powder, salt, ground turmeric, tomato paste, papaya pulp and lemon juice. Blend everything together thoroughly.

4 Add the chopped fresh green chillies and fresh coriander and stir to combine.

5 Add the chicken pieces, coating them with the marinade and making sure it goes into all the deep cuts. Cover and place it in the refrigerator to marinate for at least 4 hours.

6 When you are ready to cook, set the oven to its highest temperature. Keep a close eye on it, and don't leave the very hot oven unattended. Place the marinated chicken pieces in an ovenproof dish and pour the oil over the top. Reserve the leftover marinade in the bowl, for basting.

7 Once the oven is up to temperature, cook the chicken for 20–25 minutes, basting it with the reserved marinade several times during the cooking time, until the chicken is charred and cooked through. Keep a close eye on it.

8 Serve garnished with shredded lettuce, onion rings, sliced tomatoes, chopped fresh coriander, fresh green chillies and lemon wedges.

SERVES 4

1 medium chicken
60ml/4 tbsp whole natural (plain) yogurt
25ml/1½ tbsp garam masala
5ml/1 tsp garlic pulp
5ml/1 tsp ginger pulp
10ml/2 tsp ground cumin
10ml/2 tsp ground coriander
10ml/2 tsp chilli powder
7.5ml/1½ tsp salt
2.5ml/½ tsp ground turmeric
30ml/2 tbsp tomato paste
30ml/2 tbsp raw papaya pulp
60–90ml/4–6 tbsp lemon juice
3 fresh green chillies, very finely chopped
15ml/1 tbsp chopped fresh coriander (cilantro)
90ml/6 tbsp vegetable oil

TO GARNISH

½ small iceberg lettuce, shredded
2 red onions, peeled and sliced into rings
2 tomatoes, sliced into rounds
30ml/1 tbsp chopped fresh coriander (cilantro)
2–4 fresh green chillies
6 lemon wedges

COOK'S TIP

It is important to marinate the chicken for 4–6 hours to obtain maximum flavour.

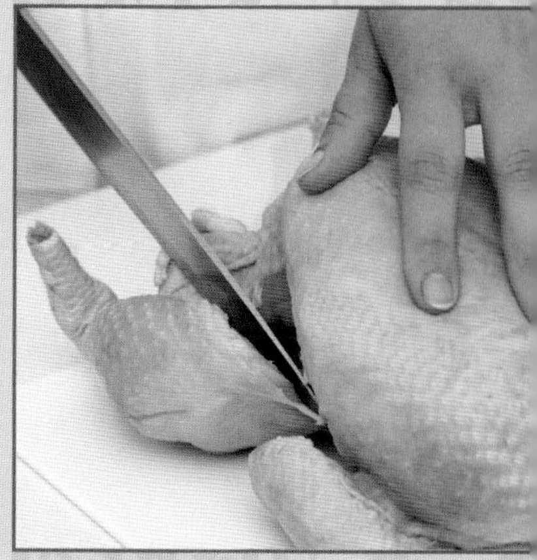

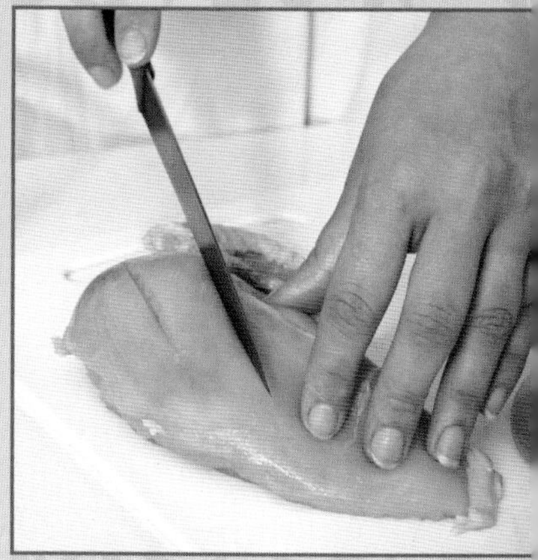

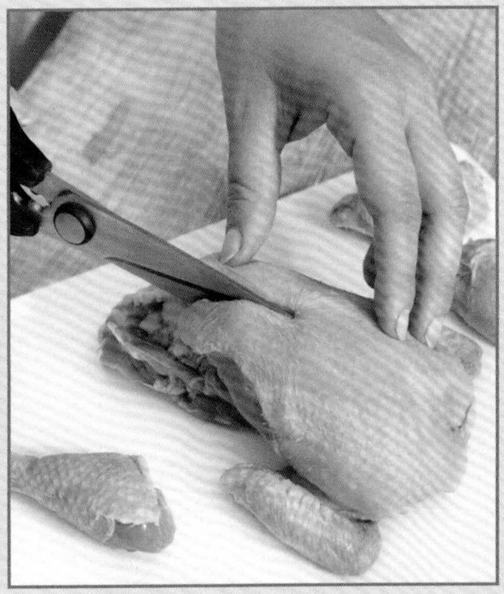

ALOO AUR NIMBOO KI MURGH

POTATO AND LEMON CHICKEN

This simple recipe is often made with lamb and is enjoyed all over Pakistan, where the native lemons are small and especially juicy, with thin lime-green and pale-yellow skins. The spiced chicken cooks at the same time as the new potatoes, making this a warming meal-in-a-bowl. In this particular recipe, I prefer chicken on the bone, but it's a personal choice.

SERVES 4

- 2 medium chicken breast fillets or 1 baby chicken, cut into 8 pieces
- 120–150ml/4fl oz–½ pint/½–⅔ cups vegetable oil
- 4–6 curry leaves
- 2.5ml/½ tsp onion seeds
- 2 medium onions, peeled and diced
- 7.5ml/1½ tsp garlic pulp
- 7.5ml/1½ tsp ginger pulp
- 10ml/2 tsp ground coriander
- 10ml/2 tsp chilli powder
- 60ml/4 tbsp lemon juice
- 15ml/1 tbsp chopped fresh coriander (cilantro)
- 2 medium potatoes, cut into slices
- 250ml/8fl oz/1 cup water
- 1 red (bell) pepper, roughly diced
- Vegetable Rice, to serve (see page 164)

1 Prepare the chicken by either cutting it into cubes, if you are using chicken breast fillets, or by jointing it into eight pieces if you are using a baby chicken. To do this, remove the legs using a sharp knife, and separate them into thighs and drumsticks. Next, use sharp kitchen scissors to cut along either side of the breastbone (discard the breastbone) and cut down the length of the underside of the chicken. Use a large sharp knife to divide each of the body halves into two. Set aside.

2 Heat the oil in a large pan with the curry leaves and onion seeds. Add the diced onions and fry over a medium heat for 10–15 minutes, until golden brown.

3 Meanwhile, blend the garlic, ginger, ground coriander and chilli powder in a large bowl with half of the lemon juice and half of the fresh coriander. Add the chicken and stir to coat the chicken well with the spice mixture.

4 Add the chicken mixture to the onions in the pan and stir-fry for 10 minutes, until the chicken is sealed all over and nearly cooked.

5 Add the sliced potatoes and water and cover the pan. Cook over a low heat for 10–15 minutes, until the potatoes are soft and the chicken is cooked through.

6 Remove the lid and stir to combine, then gently pour in the remaining lemon juice and fresh coriander and then the diced red pepper. Stir to combine, then serve hot with Vegetable Rice.

LAHORI MURGH KADAHI
LAHORI CHICKEN

This very typical, and very popular, originally Punjabi dish is a tomato-based chicken recipe that can be cooked either on or off the bone. 'Kadahi' refers to the utensil in which the chicken is cooked; this resembles a wok, although it has two small handles rather than one long one. In Pakistan, a kadahi is traditionally used to deep-fry pakoras, samosas and various other snacks and can be seen at most roadside cafes. A deep, heavy wok can be used instead.

SERVES 4

120ml/4fl oz/½ cup vegetable oil
15ml/1 tbsp vegetable ghee
10 medium tomatoes, chopped
1 onion, peeled and very finely chopped
7.5ml/1½ tsp ground coriander
10ml/2 tsp garam masala
5ml/1 tsp crushed black pepper
7.5ml/1½ tsp ground cumin
5ml/1 tsp ginger pulp
2 large chicken breast fillets, skinned and cubed
7.5ml/1½ tsp salt, or to taste
30ml/2 tbsp lemon juice
30ml/2 tbsp chopped fresh coriander (cilantro)
naan, to serve

TO GARNISH

a few sprigs fresh coriander (cilantro)
2–4 fresh whole green chillies
8–10 strips fresh peeled ginger

1 Put the oil and ghee in a wok and heat them together over a medium heat.

2 Add the chopped tomatoes and onion and cook for 3–5 minutes, until the onions are starting to soften, stirring occasionally.

3 Add the ground coriander, garam masala, crushed black pepper, ground cumin, ginger pulp, chicken pieces and salt. Lower the heat and stir-fry for about 15 minutes, until the chicken is cooked through.

4 Add the lemon juice and the chopped coriander. Stir-fry using semi-circular movements for about 10 minutes, until the oil begins to appear on the sides of the wok.

5 Transfer to a serving dish. Serve garnished with the coriander, green chillies and ginger strips. Serve with naan.

MURGH DOPIAZA
CHICKEN DOPIAZA

'Dopiaza' basically means that a dish contains twice as many onions as the main ingredient – in this case chicken, although this recipe works very well with lamb, too. Originating in southern India and brought to Pakistan by refugees, this dish also has roots in Hyderabad, although such is its appeal that it is now universally enjoyed all over Pakistan. It has a pleasant sweet taste due to the onions, and this is balanced by the tanginess of the mango powder.

SERVES 4

150–175ml/¼ pint–6fl oz/ ⅔–¾ cup vegetable oil
6 curry leaves
6 medium onions, peeled and diced
5ml/1 tsp ginger pulp
5ml/1 tsp garlic pulp
7.5ml/1½ tsp chilli powder
2.5ml/½ tsp ground turmeric
7.5ml/1½ tsp ground coriander
7.5ml/1½ tsp salt
10ml/2 tsp ground mango powder (amchoor)
1 baby chicken, skinned and cut into 8–10 pieces, or 8–10 boneless chicken portions, such as boneless chicken thighs and breast fillets
350ml/12fl oz/1½ cups water
15ml/1 tbsp chopped fresh coriander (cilantro)
rice and/or paratha, to serve

TO GARNISH

30ml/2 tbsp vegetable oil
1 onion, peeled and sliced into rings
15ml/1 tbsp chopped fresh coriander (cilantro)
4 fresh green chillies, sliced lengthwise and seeded

1 In a large pan, heat the oil with the curry leaves, then add the diced onions and fry for 7–10 minutes over a medium heat, until the onions soften and turn golden brown.

2 Meanwhile, blend together the ginger, garlic, chilli powder, ground turmeric, ground coriander, salt and ground mango powder in a large bowl, then add the chicken pieces and stir to combine well.

3 Add the chicken and spice mixture to the pan and stir-fry for about 5 minutes, until the chicken is sealed. Pour in the water and the fresh coriander, cover and cook for about 15 minutes, until the chicken is cooked. Boneless chicken will take less time to cook.

4 Once the chicken is cooked, remove the lid and simmer for 10–15 minutes, until the liquid has evaporated and you have a thick sauce.

5 Meanwhile, prepare the garnish. Heat the oil and fry the sliced onions for 10–15 minutes, until dark golden brown.

6 Transfer the dopiaza to a serving dish, add the fresh coriander and chillies and pour over the browned onions. Serve hot with rice and/or paratha.

COOK'S TIP

It is best to use include some of the more flavoursome leg or thigh meat if you choose to use boneless chicken pieces, rather than just breast fillet.

KADAHI MURGH QEEMA
FRIED MINCED CHICKEN

This minced chicken dish is cooked with tomatoes to form the base, and is garnished with crispy fried onions. Traditionally cooked in a kadahi, the ubiquitous pan once used primarily in the frontier regions and north India for deep-frying but now employed in much the same way as a wok for any type of frying, it is quick to create and as tasty as it is colourful.

SERVES 4

75ml/5 tbsp vegetable oil
5 medium tomatoes, chopped
8 curry leaves
450g/1lb minced (ground) chicken
5ml/1 tsp garlic pulp
5ml/1 tsp ginger pulp
10ml/2 tsp ground coriander
10ml/2 tsp chilli powder
7.5ml/1½ tsp salt
1 medium onion, peeled and sliced
1 green and 1 yellow (bell) pepper, seeded and thickly sliced
15ml/1 tbsp chopped fresh coriander (cilantro)

1 Heat 60ml/4 tbsp of the oil in a wok, add the tomatoes and curry leaves and stir-fry for about 5 minutes, until the tomatoes are softened.

2 Mix together the minced chicken with the garlic, ginger, ground coriander, chilli powder and salt. Add this to the tomatoes in the wok and cook for a further 7–10 minutes, stirring occasionally so the mixture doesn't catch.

3 Meanwhile, fry the sliced onions in the remaining oil in a separate frying pan over a medium-high heat for 10 minutes, until golden brown and crispy.

4 Add the sliced peppers and chopped fresh coriander to the chicken. Taste and adjust the seasoning according to your taste.

5 Once oil appears on the sides of the wok (after about 10 minutes), remove the wok from the heat and transfer the food to a serving dish. Serve decorated with the crispy onions.

PALAK MURGH
CHICKEN WITH SPINACH

This vibrant chicken dish is eaten all over the Punjab and is so popular that it is included as part of most wedding feasts. Once again, the chicken can be cooked on or off the bone, according to personal preference. Canned leaf or puréed spinach works really well in this dish, but if you prefer you can use washed, chopped fresh spinach instead, as would traditionally be used in Pakistan.

1 Heat the oil in a large pan, add the onion and fry for 10–15 minutes over a medium heat, until golden brown.

2 Add the cubed chicken along with the garam masala, ground coriander, garlic, ginger, chilli powder, turmeric and salt. Stir-fry for 3–5 minutes to seal the chicken all over.

3 Add the spinach and water. Cover the pan, lower the heat to medium and cook, stirring occasionally, for about 10 minutes.

4 Remove the lid, increase the heat and stir-fry the mixture for 10 minutes, until oil appears on the sides of the pan.

5 Add the fresh coriander and chilli, then stir in the lemon juice. Mix well to combine, then serve with plain boiled rice or chapatis.

SERVES 4

120ml/4fl oz/½ cup vegetable oil
2 medium onions, peeled and diced
2 large chicken breast fillets, cubed
7.5ml/1½ tsp garam masala
10ml/2 tsp ground coriander
7.5ml/1½ tsp garlic pulp
5ml/1 tsp ginger pulp
7.5ml/1½ tsp chilli powder
2.5ml/½ tsp ground turmeric
7.5ml/1½ tsp salt
350–400g/12–14oz fresh, frozen or canned spinach
250ml/8fl oz/1 cup water
60ml/4 tbsp chopped fresh coriander (cilantro)
2–3 fresh green chillies, sliced lengthwise and seeded
45–60ml/3–4 tbsp lemon juice
plain boiled rice or chapatis, to serve

HARA MASALA MURGH
CHICKEN WITH GREEN SPICES

Hara masala is a name given when green spices are used to flavour a dish, namely fresh coriander, mint and green chillies, and here this verdant paste is combined with other green ingredients, including lime, spring onions and green bell peppers. Originally an Indian dish, it has become very popular in Pakistan in recent years and can either be served as an appetizer or as part of a main meal.

SERVES 4

2 large skinless chicken breast fillets, cubed
10ml/2 tsp ginger pulp
5ml/1 tsp garlic pulp
2 fresh green chillies, finely chopped
45ml/3 tbsp chopped fresh coriander (cilantro)
30ml/2 tbsp mint sauce
30ml/2 tbsp lime juice
30ml/2 tbsp whole natural (plain) yogurt
7.5ml/1½ tsp salt
75ml/5 tbsp vegetable oil
6–8 spring onions (scallions), roughly chopped
250ml/8fl oz/1 cup water
1 large green (bell) pepper, seeded and diced
4–6 fresh mint leaves, roughly chopped
3 fresh green chillies, split lengthwise

FOR THE GARNISH

15ml/1 tbsp vegetable oil
6–8 shallots, peeled
6–8 cherry tomatoes
2 limes, cut into quarters

1 In a large bowl, mix together the chicken pieces with the ginger and garlic.

2 Blend together the green chillies, 15ml/1 tbsp of the fresh coriander, the mint sauce and the lime juice, then pour the mixture over the chicken pieces.

3 Mix together the yogurt and salt and set aside.

4 Heat the oil in a large frying pan over a medium heat and sauté the spring onions for about 3 minutes, until softened.

5 Add the chicken pieces to the frying pan and stir-fry for about 5 minutes to seal the chicken all over. Slowly add the yogurt and salt mixture and, still stirring, add the water.

6 Cook over a low heat for about 10 minutes, until the liquid has evaporated.

7 Add the diced pepper, fresh mint, remaining fresh coriander and fresh green chillies. Stir to combine well and remove from the heat.

8 For the garnish, heat the oil in a frying pan and fry the whole peeled shallots over a high heat for 2 minutes. Add the cherry tomatoes and fry for 3–5 minutes, until both the tomatoes and shallots are lightly charred all over.

9 Transfer the chicken mixture to a serving dish and top with the shallots and tomatoes. Serve with lime quarters.

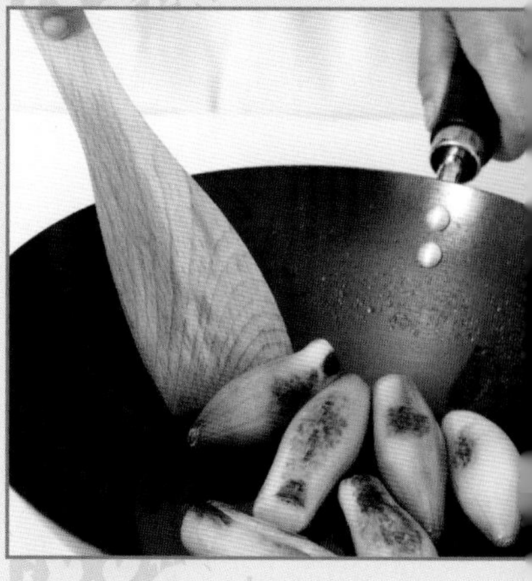

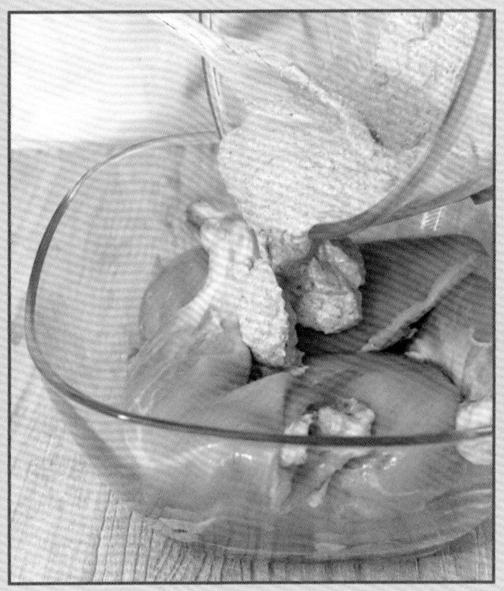

MASALA MURGH
PAKISTANI FRIED CHICKEN

Pakistanis adore fried food and it is a dominant, recurring feature on the epicurean landscape of the whole country. Aside from making the food delicious, the intense heat of the oil helps to kill any bacteria, and the quick cooking combined with the spices results in flavoursome, moist flesh.

SERVES 4

1 medium chicken
45ml/3 tbsp lemon juice
7.5ml/1½ tsp crushed dried chilli flakes
7.5ml/1½ tsp garlic pulp
7.5ml/1½ tsp ginger pulp
120ml/4fl oz/½ cup whole natural (plain) yogurt
7.5ml/1½ tsp ground cumin
7.5ml/1½ tsp ground coriander
7.5ml/1½ tsp garam masala
30ml/2 tbsp ground almonds
5ml/1 tsp salt
about 120ml/4fl oz/½ cup vegetable oil, for deep-frying

TO GARNISH

2 lemons, cut into quarter wedges
1 red onion, peeled and sliced into rings
30ml/2 tbsp chopped fresh coriander (cilantro)
8–10 mint leaves
3–4 tomatoes, sliced

1 Cut the chicken into four pieces by removing the legs using a sharp knife, then use sharp kitchen scissors to cut along either side of the breastbone (discard the breastbone) and cut down the length of the underside of the chicken so the body is in two halves. Remove the skin.

2 In a large bowl using a spoon, or with a food processor, blend together the lemon juice, crushed dried chilli flakes, garlic, ginger, yogurt, ground cumin and coriander, garam masala, ground almonds and salt.

3 Pour the mixture over the chicken and stir to combine, making sure that all of the pieces are fully coated with the mixture.

4 Pour the cooking oil into a large, deep pan or frying pan – the oil should come two-thirds of the way up the sides. Heat the oil until it reaches 180°C/350°F on a thermometer, then carefully lower each piece of chicken into the pan, gently stirring to completely submerge all of the chicken pieces in the oil.

5 Lower the heat, cover the pan with a lid and let it cook for 10–12 minutes, checking occasionally and moving the pieces around, until the chicken is golden and cooked through.

6 Once the chicken is cooked, remove the pieces from the oil using a slotted spoon and place them on a dish lined with kitchen paper. Leave to drain for just a minute, then serve hot, garnished with lemon wedges, onion rings, chopped fresh coriander, mint leaves and sliced tomatoes.

MASALA MALAIDHAAR MURGH
MASALA CREAMY CHICKEN

This mild and creamy curry only contains a little chilli powder, so it is a dish that some children will enjoy. If you prefer your curry with a little more pep, do feel free to add more chilli powder, although not so much that it masks the delicate, aromatic flavour imparted by the combination of the other spices used in the rich sauce.

SERVES 4

2 medium onions, peeled and roughly chopped
25ml/1½ tbsp ground almonds
15ml/1 tbsp coconut powder or creamed coconut
5ml/1 tsp ginger pulp
7.5ml/1½ tsp garlic pulp
7.5ml/1½ tsp ground coriander
1.5ml/¼ tsp ground mace
1.5ml/¼ tsp ground cardamom
2.5ml/½ tsp ground turmeric
10ml/2 tsp chilli powder
5ml/1 tsp salt, or to taste
45ml/3 tbsp Greek (US strained plain) yogurt
2 large skinless chicken breast fillets, cut into cubes
60–75ml/4–5 tbsp vegetable oil
75g/3oz/6 tbsp butter
120ml/4fl oz/½ cup water
30–45ml/2–3 tbsp lemon juice
60–90ml/4–6 tbsp double (heavy) cream
30ml/2 tbsp chopped fresh coriander (cilantro), to garnish
plain boiled rice or any Pakistani bread, to serve

1 Put the onion in a food processor and process to make a pulp, then set aside.

2 In a large bowl, blend together the ground almonds, coconut powder or creamed coconut, ginger and garlic along with the ground coriander, mace, cardamom, turmeric, chilli powder, salt and yogurt. Add the cubed chicken and stir to coat.

3 Heat the oil and butter in a large pan over a medium heat, then add the onion purée and fry for about 10 minutes, until golden brown, stirring occasionally.

4 Add the chicken mixture and stir to combine everything. Add the water and cook over a medium-low heat for 10–15 minutes, stirring frequently, until the chicken is cooked through, the sauce is reduced and oil begins to appear around the sides of the pan.

5 Add the lemon juice, taste and adjust the seasoning as required, then gently stir in the cream at the last minute. Do not let the cream boil or it will split.

6 Transfer to a serving dish, garnish with fresh coriander and serve with plain boiled rice or any Pakistani bread.

COOK'S TIP

Coconut powder can be bought from most Asian stores, and is a very convenient way of adding a creamy flavour and consistency to a dish. If you prefer, you can use an equal quantity of creamed coconut or coconut cream.

KASHMIRI MURGH
KASHMIRI CHICKEN WITH DRIED FRUITS

Dried fruits and nuts are primarily enjoyed during the winter months in Pakistan and especially in Kashmir and Balochistan, bringing a dash of colour and an intense fruity flavour to the table when the fresh varieties are out of season. Large golden raisins called munakka, apricots, walnuts, almonds and pistachios are especially popular, and bring a sweet element to dishes such as this Kashmiri chicken classic.

SERVES 4

- 2 large chicken breast fillets
- 1.5ml/¼ tsp ground cinnamon
- 1.5ml/¼ tsp ground allspice
- 5ml/1 tsp ground fennel seeds
- 1.5ml/¼ tsp ground cardamom
- 5ml/1 tsp ground coriander
- 1.5ml/¼ tsp ground turmeric
- 10ml/2 tsp chilli powder
- 5ml/1 tsp salt
- 7.5ml/1½ tsp ginger pulp
- 5ml/1 tsp garlic pulp
- 15ml/1 tbsp tomato paste
- 30ml/2 tbsp lemon juice
- 30ml/2 tbsp Greek (US strained plain) yogurt
- 60ml/4 tbsp vegetable oil
- 50g/2oz/¼ cup butter
- 1 bay leaf
- 2 medium onions, peeled and finely chopped
- 15ml/1 tbsp sultanas (golden raisins)
- 4–6 ready-to-eat dried apricots, quartered
- 15ml/1 tbsp cashew nuts, roughly chopped
- 45–60ml/3–4 tbsp double (heavy) cream
- 15ml/1 tbsp chopped fresh coriander (cilantro)
- 2–3 fresh red chillies, split lengthwise and seeded, to garnish
- plain boiled rice, to serve

1 Remove the skin from the chicken, cut it into even cubes and set it aside in a large mixing bowl.

2 Add the ground cinnamon, allspice, fennel seeds, cardamom, coriander, turmeric and chilli powder to the chicken, followed by the salt, ginger, garlic, tomato paste, lemon juice and yogurt and stir well to combine.

3 Cover the bowl, place it in the refrigerator and leave the chicken to marinate for 30 minutes.

4 When you are ready to cook, heat the oil and butter in a large pan over a medium heat. Add the bay leaf and onion and fry, stirring frequently, for 10–15 minutes, until the onion is golden brown.

5 Add the chicken and its marinade to the pan and stir-fry for 5–7 minutes, until the chicken is sealed. Cover with a lid, lower the heat and cook for 10 minutes, stirring frequently. You may need to add a drop of water if the mixture is sticking.

6 Add the sultanas, apricots and cashew nuts followed by the cream and half the fresh coriander and stir to combine. Cook for a further 5–10 minutes, stirring frequently, until the chicken is cooked through.

7 Stir well and transfer to a serving dish. Serve garnished with the remaining fresh coriander and the split fresh red chillies, accompanied by some plain boiled rice.

CHOLAY MURGH
CHICKEN WITH CHICKPEAS

Originating in Punjab, this wholesome dish is fairly easy to make and is simply delicious served with potatoes or plain boiled rice. I have made this curry a little different by adding some tamarind chutney, which gives it a mouthwatering tangy-yet-sweet taste, but you can omit it if you prefer to be completely authentic.

SERVES 4

2 large skinless chicken breast fillets
2 medium onions, peeled and sliced
2 medium tomatoes, sliced
7.5ml/1½ tsp ginger pulp
7.5ml/1½ tsp garlic pulp
2.5ml/½ tsp ground turmeric
10ml/2 tsp chilli powder
7.5ml/1½ tsp ground cumin
10ml/2 tsp ground coriander
5–7.5ml/1–1½ tsp salt
30ml/2 tbsp lemon juice
90–120ml/6–8 tbsp vegetable oil
1.5ml/¼ tsp onion seeds
4 curry leaves
15ml/1 tbsp tamarind chutney
30ml/2 tbsp chopped fresh coriander (cilantro)
120–175ml/4–6fl oz/½–¾ cup water
200g/7oz canned chickpeas, drained
2 fresh green chillies, chopped
boiled potatoes or plain boiled rice, to serve

1 Trim off any fat from the chicken breast fillets and cut them into bitesize cubes.

2 Put the sliced onion and tomato in a food processor or blender and process until quite finely chopped.

3 Add the ginger, garlic, ground turmeric, chilli powder, ground cumin, ground coriander, salt and lemon juice and blend for about 1 minute more.

4 Heat the oil in a large frying pan and fry the onion seeds and curry leaves for about 1 minute, until aromatic. Add the onion and spice mixture and stir-fry for 3–5 minutes over a medium heat, stirring frequently, until the onion just starts to soften.

5 Add the tamarind chutney and mix everything together, then add the chicken and stir-fry for a further 2 minutes to seal the meat. Add half the fresh coriander and all of the water, cover and cook for 7 minutes.

6 Stir in the chickpeas and cook for 7–10 minutes more, until the sauce is fairly thick. If it is not, cook it for a further 2–3 minutes, stirring gently.

7 Stir in the remaining fresh coriander and the green chillies, then serve with boiled potatoes or plain boiled rice.

LAHORI MURGH CHARGHA

LAHORI STEAMED CHICKEN

Heralding from Lahore, the capital of Punjab and the second-most populated city in Pakistan, this spicy dish tastes as good as it looks. Making it involves several cooking methods, with the baby chicken being marinated for a couple of hours before being steam-cooked and finally fried in a deep wok until it is golden brown. It is best to use a baby chicken as it is much easier to cook and manage during the frying stage than a larger bird.

SERVES 4

1 whole baby chicken
90ml/6 tbsp lemon juice
30ml/2 tbsp chilli powder
25ml/1½ tbsp garlic pulp
25ml/1½ tbsp ginger pulp
30ml/2 tbsp whole natural (plain) yogurt
7.5ml/½ tbsp ground cinnamon
2.5ml/½ tsp ground turmeric
12.5ml/2½ tsp ground coriander
12.5ml/2½ tsp garam masala
5ml/1 tsp soft light brown sugar
7.5ml/1½ tsp salt
60ml/4 tbsp chaat masala
vegetable oil, for deep-frying

TO SERVE

3–4 tomatoes, sliced
1 red onion, peeled and sliced into rings or 3–4 spring onions (scallions), split lengthwise
2 fresh green chillies, split lengthwise
1 lemon, cut into wedges

1 Remove the skin from the baby chicken. Using a sharp knife, make several deep cuts on the drumsticks and breasts.

2 In a large bowl, mix together the remaining ingredients, apart from the oil and using just half of the chaat masala, to form a paste.

3 Spread the chicken with the paste, completely covering it and ensuring you work it into the deep cuts. Place the chicken in the bowl, cover it and leave it to marinate in the refrigerator for 2 hours.

4 To steam the chicken, place it on a trivet in a deep pan, pour in boiling water to a depth of about 5cm/2in, cover with a lid and steam-cook on the hob for 25–30 minutes.

5 Two-thirds fill a deep wok or pan with oil and heat until it reaches 180°C/350°F on a thermometer. Carefully lower the steamed chicken into the hot oil using tongs or a slotted spoon, ensuring the chicken is submerged. Fry for 15 minutes, until golden brown and cooked through.

6 Carefully lift out the fried chicken to a plate lined with kitchen paper using tongs or a slotted spoon. Leave the fried chicken to drain for about 1 minute, then sprinkle it with the rest of the chaat masala. Serve with a Pakistani salad of sliced tomatoes, onion rings or spring onions, green chillies and lemon wedges.

VARIATION Instead of steaming the marinated chicken over water, you can place it on a piece of oiled foil, fold up the sides to make a loose but tightly sealed parcel and then bake it in a 180°C/350°F/Gas 4 oven for 20–25 minutes.

MALAI MURGH TIKKA

MALAI CHICKEN TIKKA

Once tasted, never forgotten, this popular dish can be served as an appetizer or as part of the main meal and will appeal to children and those who don't like their food too spicy. 'Malai' means 'creamy', and this aspect is lent to the dish by the inclusion of lashings of butter along with a few spoonfuls of thick yogurt. If you are feeling really decadent, you could substitute the latter with thick cream.

SERVES 4

75g/3oz/6 tbsp butter
2.5ml/½ tsp ground turmeric
7.5ml/1½ tsp ground coriander
7.5ml/1½ tsp garam masala
10ml/2 tsp chilli powder
5ml/1 tsp paprika
10ml/2 tsp garlic pulp
10ml/2 tsp ginger pulp
30ml/2 tbsp tomato paste
45ml/3 tbsp Greek (US strained plain) yogurt
7.5ml/1½ tsp salt
20ml/4 tsp lemon juice
15ml/1 tbsp chopped fresh coriander (cilantro)
3 skinless chicken breast fillets, diced into cubes
30ml/2 tbsp vegetable oil, for basting

TO GARNISH

1 red onions, peeled and sliced into rings
2 fresh green chillies, split lengthwise
15ml/1 tbsp chopped fresh coriander (cilantro)
a few drops of lemon juice
lemon wedges

1 Melt the butter in a medium pan, then whisk in all the ground spices along with the garlic, ginger, tomato paste, yogurt, salt, lemon juice and the fresh coriander and blend everything together.

2 Put the cubed chicken in a large bowl and pour over the butter and spice mixture. Mix thoroughly, cover the bowl and leave to marinate in the refrigerator for at least 3 hours.

3 When you are ready to cook, preheat the grill or broiler to high. Mix everything again, then place the chicken in a grill-proof dish.

4 Grill the chicken, turning it over once or twice and basting it with oil to ensure even cooking, for about 20–25 minutes or until the chicken is cooked through and lightly charred. The charring is important, so keep the chicken under the highest heat until you achieve this result. Keep a close eye on the chicken towards the end of the cooking time.

5 Transfer the cooked chicken to a serving dish and serve garnished with onion rings, split green chillies and fresh coriander. Sprinkle over a little lemon juice and serve with lemon wedges.

ACHARI MURGH

CHICKEN COOKED WITH PICKLING SPICES

Numerous whole spices are used for this Pakistani classic, as may be expected for a dish whose Urdu name translates as 'pickled and seasoned with spices'. It is usually made with chicken on the bone for added flavour, but you can also use chicken breast fillets if you prefer.

SERVES 4

1 baby chicken or 2 large skinless chicken breast fillets
60–75ml/4–5 tbsp vegetable oil
1.5ml/¼ tsp mustard seeds
1.5ml/¼ tsp onion seeds
4 fenugreek seeds
1.5ml/¼ tsp fennel seeds
6 curry leaves
1 medium onion, peeled and finely diced
5ml/1 tsp ginger pulp
5ml/1 tsp garlic pulp
5ml/1 tsp ground cumin
1.5ml/¼ tsp ground turmeric
10ml/2 tsp chilli powder
5ml/1 tsp crushed dried chilli flakes
5ml/1 tsp salt, or to taste
2.5ml/½ tsp crushed coriander seeds
30ml/2 tbsp tamarind sauce
30ml/2 tbsp lemon juice
250ml/8fl oz/1 cup water
15ml/1 tbsp chopped fresh coriander (cilantro)
plain boiled rice, to serve

TO GARNISH

4–5 fresh green chillies
30ml/2 tbsp vegetable oil
15ml/1 tbsp chopped fresh coriander (cilantro)
7.5ml/1½ tsp chaat masala (optional)

1 If you are using a whole baby chicken, remove the skin and joint it into eight pieces (two wings, two drumsticks, two thighs and two breasts on the bone). Alternatively, for off-the-bone curry, cut the chicken breast fillets into cubes.

2 Heat the oil in a large pan or wok over a medium heat and add all the seeds and the curry leaves. Fry for about 1 minute, until the spices release their aroma, then add the chopped onion and fry for about 10 minutes, stirring frequently, until golden brown.

3 Meanwhile, in a large bowl, thoroughly mix together the ginger, garlic, ground cumin, ground turmeric, chilli powder, crushed dried chilli flakes, salt, crushed coriander seeds and the tamarind sauce.

4 Stir in the lemon juice, then add the chicken pieces to the bowl and stir to coat thoroughly.

5 Add the chicken to the pan of frying onions and stir to combine, then add the water. Reduce the heat to low, cover the pan with a lid and let the chicken cook for 10–15 minutes, checking it occasionally to ensure that it does not catch on the bottom of the pan.

6 Stir in the fresh coriander, re-cover and simmer for about 7 minutes. Remove the lid and stir-fry for 5–8 minutes to drive off moisture and produce a thick sauce, and tender, completely cooked chicken. Remove the pan from the heat and transfer the chicken to a serving dish.

7 For the garnish, slit the green chillies lengthwise, remove the seeds and shallow-fry them in the oil for 2 minutes. Pour the chillies and the oil over the chicken, sprinkle over the fresh coriander and the chaat masala (if using) and serve with plain boiled rice.

KAT-A-KAT MURGH
KAT-A-KAT CHICKEN

Like everywhere else in the world, Pakistan has had its share of food trends. This particular recipe, whose origins lie in Karachi and Sindh, has gained popularity throughout the country and even internationally in the last 15 years or so. Kat-a-kat or tak-a-tak is a special meat dish traditionally made from offal – including brain, kidney and heart – and lamb chops or chopped shoulder or leg of lamb, in combination with various spices, yogurt and tomatoes cooked in butter. This version caters for those who are not keen on offal, and uses chicken in its place, but you could also use finely chopped boneless lamb. The dish's name is onomatopoeic, describing the sound of the two sharp blades that hit the griddle as they cut up the meat into very small pieces while it is cooking. Traditionally cooked on a large griddle or tawa, similar to the one used for making chapatis, it works just as well in a large frying pan or skillet.

SERVES 4

30ml/2 tbsp whole natural (plain) yogurt
7.5ml/1½ tsp ginger pulp
7.5ml/1½ tsp garlic pulp
90–120ml/6–8 tbsp vegetable oil
2 medium onions, peeled and finely chopped
3 medium tomatoes, chopped
½ bunch fresh fenugreek leaves
7.5ml/1½ tsp garam masala
7.5ml/1½ tsp chilli powder
7.5ml/1½ tsp ground coriander
2.5ml/½ tsp ground black pepper
2.5ml/½ tsp ground cinnamon
1.5ml/¼ tsp ground cardamom seeds
1.5ml/¼ tsp citric acid or 5ml/1 tsp lemon juice
1 whole baby chicken, skinned, boned and cut into very small pieces
60ml/4 tbsp chopped fresh coriander (cilantro)
2.5cm/½in fresh root ginger, peeled and cut into strips
2 each fresh red and green chillies, split lengthwise and seeded
naan, to serve

1 Mix together the yogurt, ginger and garlic and set aside.

2 Heat the oil in a large frying pan over a medium heat, then add the onion, tomatoes and fenugreek leaves and fry together for 7–10 minutes, stirring occasionally, until the onion is softened.

3 Slowly add the garam masala and chilli powder along with the ground coriander, black pepper, cinnamon, cardamom seeds and the citric acid or lemon juice and fry for a further 5 minutes.

4 Add the chicken pieces along with 15ml/1 tbsp of the fresh coriander. Reduce the heat to low. Stir-fry, chopping the chicken pieces down as you cook them, for 10–15 minutes, until the liquid has evaporated and the chicken is cooked.

5 Add the remaining fresh coriander, ginger strips and fresh chillies and cover the pan for 2–3 minutes. Remove the lid and serve hot with naan.

MEAT

RECIPES

KEEMA METHI

MINCED LAMB WITH FRESH FENUGREEK

Originating in the south-eastern Indian province of Andhra Pradesh, keema methi and other dishes made with ground lamb (keema) are very economical, which, along with the fact that they are delicious and quick to make, explains why they are so popular all over Pakistan. Fresh fenugreek (methi) is the dominant flavour note in this recipe, lending a pleasant aromatic taste and vibrant colour as well as conferring numerous health benefits to the eater, such as lowering blood cholesterol, controlling blood-sugar levels and aiding digestion.

SERVES 4

60–90ml/4–6 tbsp vegetable oil
4 curry leaves
2 onions, peeled and chopped
4 tomatoes, chopped
30ml/2 tbsp fresh fenugreek, leaves only (see Cook's Tip)
5ml/1 tsp ginger pulp
7.5ml/1½ tsp garlic pulp
7.5ml/1½ tsp chilli powder
2.5ml/½ tsp ground turmeric
5–7.5ml/1–1½ tsp salt
5ml/1 tsp ground coriander
500g/1¼lb/2¼ cups finely minced (ground) leg of lamb (see Cook's Tip)
15ml/1 tbsp chopped fresh coriander (cilantro)
2–3 fresh green chillies, split lengthwise
plain boiled rice, chapatis or parathas, to serve

1 Heat the oil in a large wok over a medium heat and fry the curry leaves, onion, tomato and fenugreek leaves for 5–7 minutes, stirring frequently, until the onion starts to soften.

2 Stir in the ginger, garlic, chilli powder, ground turmeric, salt and ground coriander, followed by the lamb. Turn up the heat slightly and continue to stir-fry for 15–20 minutes, until the liquid has evaporated and oil begins to appear on the sides of the pan.

3 Add half the fresh coriander and half of the fresh chillies and mix these in.

4 Transfer to a serving dish and garnish with the remaining fresh coriander and chillies. Serve with plain boiled rice, chapatis or parathas.

COOK'S TIPS

- I always have the meat especially ground for me at a butchers from leg of lamb with as much fat removed as possible, and also ask the butcher to put it through the mincing machine at least twice so it is very finely ground.
- When picking fenugreek leaves from their stalks, be careful not to include any flowers as these can be quite bitter – you just want the leaves.

PASANDA GOSHTH
LAMB PASANDA

A very Mughlai dish, pasanda goshth is a firm favourite in many Pakistani households, especially in Karachi. This traditional recipe calls for tender cubes of lamb, which are flattened out by being vigorously bashed with a wooden tenderizer either by the butcher or at home. This treatment, in combination with the yogurt marinade, tenderizes the meat and results in a meltingly soft and succulent finished result. The addition of ground almonds and coconut milk thickens and enrichens the sauce, balancing out the heat from the chillies.

SERVES 4

450g/1lb boneless leg of lamb, trimmed and cubed
90ml/6 tbsp whole natural (plain) yogurt
5ml/1 tsp poppy seeds
30ml/2 tbsp ground almonds
30ml/2 tbsp coconut milk
7.5ml/1½ tsp ginger pulp
7.5ml/1½ tsp garlic pulp
7.5ml/1½ tsp chilli powder
5ml/1 tsp garam masala
7.5ml/1½ tsp ground coriander
15ml/1 tbsp vegetable oil
45ml/3 tbsp vegetable ghee
1.25cm/½in cinnamon stick
6 green cardamoms
4–6 black peppercorns
1.5ml/¼ tsp black cumin seeds
2 medium onions, peeled and chopped
475ml/16fl oz/2 cups water
10ml/2 tsp chopped fresh coriander (cilantro)
2 fresh green and 2 fresh red chillies, slit lengthwise and seeded (if liked)
30ml/2 tbsp lemon juice
plain boiled rice and any bread, to serve

1 To prepare the lamb, place it between two sheets of clear film (plastic wrap) or in a clean, strong plastic bag and bash it with a wooden meat mallet or a rolling pin until it is 1cm/½in thick. Alternatively, you can ask your butcher to do this for you, if you prefer.

2 In a large bowl, mix together the yogurt, poppy seeds, ground almonds, coconut milk, ginger, garlic, chilli powder, garam masala and ground coriander. Add the lamb and stir to combine thoroughly.

3 Cover the bowl and leave the meat to marinate in the refrigerator for a few hours, or ideally overnight as this will allow enough time for the lamb to absorb as much flavour as possible, as well as tenderizing the meat.

4 Heat the oil and ghee together in a large pan over a medium heat. Add the cinnamon, cardamoms, peppercorns and black cumin seeds, followed by the chopped onion. Fry for 5–7 minutes, stirring occasionally, until the onion is starting to soften.

5 Add the marinated meat and any leftover marinade to the pan and stir-fry for 5–7 minutes to seal the meat. Add the water, reduce the heat, cover the pan and cook over a low heat for 20–25 minutes, checking occasionally and stirring to prevent the mixture from sticking.

6 When the water has evaporated, check whether the lamb is tender using the point of a sharp knife; if not, add more water and cook it for a little longer. Remove the lid and stir-fry using semi-circular movements until the sauce is really thick and reduced.

7 Add half the fresh coriander and half of the chillies. Stir in the lemon juice and transfer to a serving dish. Garnish with the remaining coriander and chillies and serve with plain boiled rice and bread.

COOK'S TIP

Vegetable ghee is pure refined palm oil. It is less fatty than pure ghee and lacks the latter's sometimes pungent smell, although it has the same consistency. It is available in big tubs and cans in Asian stores.

DAAL GOSHTH

MUTTON COOKED WITH LENTILS

I use two different types of daal for this aromatic dish, which is enjoyed everywhere in Pakistan. Lentils are cheap and nutritious as well as being tasty, and bulk out the mutton to make the dish stretch further. The soft, sweet onions of the tarka garnish add the final flourish, a sweet counterpoint to the heat of the whole green chillies.

SERVES 4

120–150ml/4fl oz–¼ pint/½–⅔ cup vegetable oil
2 medium onions, peeled and sliced
450g/1lb boneless leg of mutton, trimmed of fat and cubed
10ml/2 tsp ginger pulp
10ml/2 tsp garlic pulp
10ml/2 tsp garam masala
10ml/2 tsp chilli powder
7.5ml/1½ tsp ground coriander
7.5ml/1½ tsp salt
115g/4oz/½ cup chana daal, rinsed and soaked in water for 1 hour
225g/8oz/1 cup masoor daal, rinsed and soaked in water for 1 hour
475–750ml/16fl oz–1¼ pints/2–3 cups water
45ml/3 tbsp chopped fresh coriander (cilantro)
3–4 whole green chillies, to garnish
30ml/2 tbsp lemon juice
plain boiled rice, to serve

FOR THE TARKA

45ml/3 tbsp vegetable oil
1 medium onion, peeled and sliced
2.5ml/½ tsp white cumin seeds

1 Heat the oil in a large pan over a medium heat and fry the sliced onions for 10–15 minutes, until golden brown.

2 Add the mutton along with the ginger, garlic, garam masala, chilli powder, ground coriander and salt and stir-fry for 3–5 minutes, to seal the meat.

3 Drain the chana daal and masoor daal and add them to the pan. Stir to combine, then add the water and half the fresh coriander and cook for about 20–30 minutes, stirring using semi-circular movements, until the lamb is tender and the water has evaporated. Transfer to a serving dish and keep warm.

4 Make the tarka in a separate frying pan. Heat the oil over a medium heat and fry the onion with the whole cumin seeds for about 10 minutes, until the onions are golden.

5 Pour the tarka over the lamb. Garnish with the remaining fresh coriander and the fresh green chillies. Sprinkle the lemon juice over the top and serve with plain boiled rice.

BHUNA GOSHTH
LAMB BHUNA

Originally from the Bengal region of north-eastern India and subsequently northern Pakistan, bhuna refers to the method of stir-frying a dish using semi-circular movements until the oil separates out and the sauce forms a thick paste. This intensifies the flavours and produces a delectable end result. When using lamb for any recipe, always make sure it is the best quality available and remove as much of the fat as possible. Lamb on the bone is best for this recipe as it gives the most flavoursome end result, but if this isn't available then boneless meat is fine.

SERVES 4

90–120ml/6–8 tbsp vegetable oil
3 medium onions, peeled and chopped
7.5ml/1½ tsp ginger pulp
7.5ml/1½ tsp garlic pulp
7.5ml/1½ tsp ground cumin
5ml/1 tsp garam masala
10ml/2 tsp chilli powder
5ml/1 tsp salt, or to taste
45ml/3 tbsp whole natural (plain) yogurt
450g/1lb leg of lamb, on the bone, cut into small pieces (ask your butcher to do this with a cleaver)
475ml/16fl oz/2 cups water
1 large green (bell) pepper, seeded and sliced
2 medium tomatoes, quartered
45ml/3 tbsp chopped fresh coriander (cilantro)
30ml/2 tbsp lemon juice
5ml/1 tsp fresh mint, to garnish
1–2 fresh green chillies, sliced (seeded if preferred), to garnish
plain boiled rice and chapatis, to serve

1 Heat the oil in a large pan over a medium heat, add half the onions and fry for 10–15 minutes, until soft and golden brown.

2 Meanwhile, mix together the ginger, garlic, ground cumin, garam masala, chilli powder, salt and yogurt in a large bowl. Add the lamb and mix to combine well.

3 Once the onions are golden brown, add the meat mixture to the pan and stir-fry for 5–7 minutes, to seal the meat.

4 Add the water, cover and cook over a medium heat for 20–25 minutes, or until the meat is cooked and tender and all the water is evaporate.

5 Remove the lid and start to stir-fry using semi-circular movements, for about 10 minutes or until the oil begins to separate.

6 Add the remaining onion, pepper, tomatoes and fresh coriander and continue to stir-fry for a further 5–7 minutes.

7 Sprinkle with the lemon juice, then transfer to a serving dish and garnish with the remaining coriander, the mint and sliced fresh chillies. Serve with plain boiled rice and chapatis.

GOBI GOSHTH

LAMB AND CAULIFLOWER CURRY WITH PEPPERS

Sold at bustling markets all over Pakistan, the simla mirch (bell peppers) and pul gobi (cauliflowers) in gobi goshth add flavour, colour and texture as well as their nutritional benefits, and help to bulk out the more costly meat. Perhaps as a result of the relative paucity of water, peppers grown in Pakistan tend to be smaller than those sold in the West, but have an intense flavour that lends a sweet, aromatic note to dishes.

SERVES 4

120ml/4fl oz/½ cup vegetable oil
2 medium onions, peeled and diced
450g/1lb boned leg of lamb, trimmed and diced
5ml/1 tsp ginger pulp
5ml/1 tsp garlic pulp
7.5ml/1½ tsp chilli powder
1.5ml/¼ tsp ground turmeric
5–7.5ml/1–1½ tsp salt
1 small cauliflower, cut into medium pieces
475ml/16fl oz/2 cups water
10ml/2 tsp lemon juice
1 green and 1 red (bell) pepper, seeded and roughly diced
2.5ml/½ tsp onion seeds
6 curry leaves
30ml/2 tbsp chopped fresh coriander (cilantro), to garnish
plain boiled rice or chapatis, to serve

1 Heat 90ml/6 tbsp of the oil in a medium pan over a medium heat. Add the onion and fry for 10–15 minutes, until soft and golden brown.

2 Add the cubed lamb and fry for 3–4 minutes, to seal the meat.

3 Add the ginger, garlic, chilli powder, ground turmeric and salt and stir to combine well. Add half the cauliflower and all of the water. Reduce the heat to low, cover and cook for about 45 minutes, stirring occasionally to make sure it does not stick on the bottom of the pan.

4 Check the lamb is tender using the point of a knife, then remove the lid and stir-fry for about 7 minutes, using semi-circular movements and scraping the bottom of the pan, until the sauce is thick and the oil separates.

5 Pour in the lemon juice and adjust the seasoning according to your taste. Remove from the heat and transfer to a serving dish.

6 Heat the remaining oil and fry the sliced peppers and the remaining cauliflower with the onion seeds and curry leaves for about 5 minutes, until the vegetables are softened slightly.

7 Pour the pepper and cauliflower mixture over the lamb. Garnish with the fresh coriander and serve with plain boiled rice or chapatis.

MUTTON KUNNA
SLOW-COOKED MUTTON STEW

This rich and irresistible curry is quite similar to nehari and originates from the region of Chiniot, in Punjab, which is also known for its intricately carved wooden furniture. It is cooked slowly and flour is added at the end to produce a thick sauce, which can be scooped up with naan. Traditionally, kunna is made using a stock based on sheep's trotters, an economical as well as a practical custom that results in a slightly gelatinous cooking liquor that helps to thicken the stew. However, this is not absolutely necessary and you can just use a stock (bouillon) cube instead.

SERVES 4

1kg/2¼lb mutton leg
2 medium onions
75–90ml/5–6 tbsp vegetable ghee
10ml/2 tsp ginger pulp
10ml/2 tsp garlic pulp
10ml/2 tsp chilli powder
2.5ml/½ tsp ground turmeric
10ml/2 tsp salt
45ml/3 tbsp whole natural (plain) yogurt
475–750ml/16fl oz–1¼ pints/2–3 cups stock, made with trotters (see Cook's Tip) or 1 lamb stock (bouillon) cube
30ml/2 tbsp plain (all-purpose) flour
naan, to serve

FOR THE SPICE MIX

4 whole cloves
6 green cardamoms
15ml/1 tbsp white cumin seeds
15ml/1 tbsp coriander seeds
15ml/1 tbsp whole black peppercorns
2.5ml/½ tsp ground mace
2.5ml/½ tsp ground allspice

FOR THE GARNISH

2.5cm/1in fresh root ginger, peeled and sliced
30ml/2 tbsp chopped fresh coriander (cilantro)
2 each fresh green and red chillies, split lengthwise

1 Begin by making the spice mix for this curry by blending the whole spices in a grinder until they are powdered. Mix these with the ground mace and allspice and set aside.

2 Trim the leg of mutton of excess fat, then cut it into large pieces and set aside.

3 Peel and roughly chop the onions, then process them in a food processor until they are pulped.

4 In a large pan, heat the ghee over a medium-high heat then add the prepared meat and fry for 5–7 minutes, until sealed and browned all over.

5 Add the ginger and garlic and continue to stir-fry for 2–3 minutes, then add the chilli powder, ground turmeric and salt. Blend everything together, then mix in the prepared spice mixture followed by the onion pulp and stir-fry everything for 3–5 minutes.

6 Whisk the yogurt and pour it into the pan. Stir to combine, then bring the mixture to the boil and pour in enough stock to cover. Turn down the heat to medium and cook for about 1 hour, until the mutton is very tender and the gravy is thick.

7 Lower the heat, then slake the flour in about 250ml/8fl oz/1 cup water and pour this on to the curry to thicken the sauce. Cook, stirring, for about 5 minutes, until the flour is cooked out and the sauce is thick.

8 Taste and adjust the seasoning if necessary, then transfer to a serving dish. Garnish with ginger slices, fresh coriander and chillies and serve with naan.

COOK'S TIP

If you are going to use trotters to make stock, put these in a pan with enough water to cover and slow-cook them over a low heat for about 2 hours, or until the liquid has reduced to give you about 475–750ml/16fl oz–1¼ pints/2–3 cups of stock. Strain, then set aside.

MUTTON QORMA

MUTTON CURRY WITH KEWRA WATER

Qorma is usually quite spicy and is popular at weddings and other special occasions, as well as for a main meal at other times. It takes a little longer to cook than many other curries, especially when it is made using mutton, but this results in a rich and aromatic dish with a thick gravy. It can also be made using lamb or chicken, which will reduce the cooking time, and freezes beautifully, so you could make double the quantity and freeze half for another time.

SERVES 4

90ml/6 tbsp vegetable oil
45ml/3 tbsp vegetable ghee
3 cloves
6 black peppercorns
1 bay leaf
6 green cardamoms
2.5cm/1in piece of cinnamon stick
3 medium onions, peeled, chopped and pulped in a food processor
500g/1¼lb leg of mutton, on the bone, cubed (ask your butcher to do this)
7.5ml/1½ tsp chilli powder
7.5ml/1½ tsp ginger pulp
5ml/1 tsp garlic pulp
7.5ml/1½ tsp ground coriander
5ml/1 tsp garam masala
30ml/2 tbsp coconut powder
5–7.5ml/1–1½ tsp salt
60ml/4 tbsp whole natural (plain) yogurt
0.6ml/⅛ tsp freshly grated nutmeg
0.6ml/⅛ tsp ground mace
15ml/1 tbsp kewra water
15ml/1 tbsp chopped fresh coriander, to garnish
2 fresh green chillies, chopped, to garnish
naan or parathas, to serve

1 Heat the oil and ghee in a large pan over a medium heat. Add the cloves, peppercorns, bay leaf, cardamoms and cinnamon and fry for about 2 minutes.

2 Add a quarter of the onion pulp and fry for about 7 minutes, until golden brown. Add the mutton and stir-fry for 5–7 minutes to seal the meat all over.

3 Add the chilli powder, ginger, garlic, ground coriander, garam masala, coconut powder and salt. Stir-fry for 2 minutes, then add the yogurt and stir to blend it all well. Cover and cook for 10–12 minutes.

4 Add the nutmeg, mace and kewra water, cover with a lid and cook over a medium heat for 35–45 minutes, until the meat is tender.

5 Stir to make sure the sauce is quite thick, then taste and adjust the seasoning as necessary.

6 Transfer to a serving dish and serve garnished with fresh coriander and green chillies with freshly made naan or parathas.

COOK'S TIP

Kewra water is made from pandanus flowers and is used in a similar way to rose or orange blossom extract. It is usually available from Asian stores or online.

ALOO GOSHTH

POTATOES WITH MUTTON

Potatoes and mutton go very well together, and this particular recipe for aloo goshth has a rich spicy sauce. It takes a little while to cook, but it is so delicious it is definitely worth waiting for. A regular in most households, especially Punjabi ones, it is served with freshly made chapatis or plain boiled rice. Daal makhani goes well with this too, as an accompaniment.

SERVES 4

- 105ml/7 tbsp vegetable oil
- 45–60ml/2–3 tbsp vegetable ghee
- 2 medium onions, peeled and finely chopped
- 7.5ml/1½ tsp ginger pulp
- 7.5ml/1½ tsp garlic pulp
- 10ml/2 tsp chilli powder
- 10ml/2 tsp ground coriander
- 2.5ml/½ tsp ground turmeric
- 5ml/1 tsp paprika
- 7.5ml/1½ tsp salt
- 4 medium tomatoes, chopped
- 500g/1¼lb mutton on the bone, cut into 5cm/2in cubes
- 350ml/12fl oz/1½ cups whole natural (plain) yogurt
- 12.5ml/2½ tsp garam masala
- 30–45ml/2–3 tbsp chopped fresh coriander (cilantro)
- 400ml/14fl oz/1⅔ cups water
- 8 small potatoes, peeled and halved
- 2–3 fresh green chillies
- 15ml/1 tbsp lemon juice
- freshly made chapatis, plain boiled rice or any rotis

1 Heat the oil and ghee together in a medium pan. Add the onions and fry for 10–15 minutes, until they turn a soft golden brown colour.

2 Add the ginger, garlic, chilli powder, ground coriander, ground turmeric, paprika and salt and stir-fry over a medium heat for 5–7 minutes. Add the chopped tomatoes and continue to stir-fry for a further 5–7 minutes.

3 Add the mutton, stir-fry for 2–3 minutes to blend everything together, then cook for 7–10 minutes, stirring occasionally. Pour in the yogurt and continue to cook for a further 5 minutes.

4 Add half the garam masala and half the fresh coriander followed by 150ml/¼ pint/⅔ cup of the water. Cover with a lid and cook for about 40–45 minutes, checking and stirring occasionally. Remove the lid and check that the mutton pieces are tender by piercing one with a sharp knife; it should cut fairly easily.

5 Add the potatoes, stir to combine, then add the remaining 250ml/8fl oz/1 cup water. Cook, covered with a lid, for about 15 minutes, or until the potatoes are cooked through.

6 Stir in the fresh chillies, the remaining fresh coriander and garam masala and cook for a further 5–6 minutes, or until oil appears around the edge of the pan. Taste and adjust the seasoning according to your taste.

7 Transfer to a serving dish, sprinkle over the lemon juice and serve hot with freshly made chapatis, plain boiled rice or any other rotis of your choice.

MUTTON HALEEM
MASHED MUTTON WITH CRUSHED WHEAT AND OATS

A slow-cooked dish that can feature mutton, beef or chicken, haleem is widely eaten all over Pakistan and is a favourite in the holy month of Ramadan. It consists of a meat or chicken qorma (curry) that is cooked until it is sufficiently soft to be mashed, at which point crushed wheat grains, oats and chana daal are added. This produces a very thick and flavoursome paste, which is served with a number of garnishes in separate dishes, including sliced ginger, fried onions, ghee, fresh coriander, mint and fresh green chillies. Diners help themselves to these toppings, personalizing the dish to suit their palates. Neither bread nor rice are usually served with haleem, except in Punjab, where people tend to eat it with naan.

SERVES 4

75g/3oz/½ cup crushed wheat grains
75g/3oz/½ cup chana daal
500g/1¼lb boneless mutton shoulder, trimmed and diced into small cubes
10ml/2 tsp ginger pulp
10ml/2 tsp garlic pulp
10ml/2 tsp garam masala
2.5ml/½ tsp ground cardamom
10ml/2 tsp chilli powder
10ml/2 tsp ground coriander
2.5cm/1in piece of cinnamon stick
25ml/1½ tbsp ground almonds
10ml/2 tsp salt
225g/8oz/1 cup whole natural (plain) yogurt, whisked
30ml/2 tbsp vegetable oil
120–150ml/4fl oz–¼ pint/½–⅔ cup vegetable ghee
3 medium onions, peeled and chopped
475ml/16fl oz/2 cups water
1–2 fresh green chillies, chopped
15ml/1 tbsp chopped fresh coriander (cilantro)
90g/3½oz/1 cup rolled oats

FOR THE GARNISH

120ml/4fl oz/½ cup vegetable ghee
30ml/2 tbsp dried onions
10–12 fresh root ginger slices
2–3 fresh green chillies
15ml/1 tbsp fresh coriander (cilantro) leaves
4–6 lemon wedges
2.5ml/½ tsp chaat masala
6–8 mint leaves

1 Soak the crushed wheat grains and the chana daal in a large bowl of cold water for about an hour while you prepare the ingredients for the qorma.

2 Put the mutton cubes in a large bowl. Add the ginger, garlic, garam masala, ground cardamom, chilli powder, ground coriander, cinnamon, ground almonds and salt and blend these in well with the mutton. Add the whisked yogurt and mix everything together.

3 Heat the oil and vegetable ghee in a large pan over a medium heat. Add the onions and fry for 10–15 minutes, until golden brown.

4 Add the mutton and the yogurt mixture and stir-fry for 7–10 minutes, until the meat is sealed. Pour in the water and stir to mix, then add the green chillies and the fresh coriander.

5 Cover with a lid and cook over a medium heat for about 45 minutes, stirring occasionally and making sure it does not catch at the bottom. Check the mutton is soft and tender and cooked through; the sauce should be thick and the meat soft enough to be mashed down.

6 Remove from the heat, leave to cool slightly then mash the meat with a masher or in a food processor for about 1–2 minutes, until it is smooth and paste-like. Return the paste to the large pan and set aside, off the heat.

7 Meanwhile, drain the wheat and daal and place in a large pan with the rolled oats and water to cover. Boil for about 15 minutes, until soft enough to be mashed. Transfer to a food processor and process until smooth.

8 Add this paste to the meat qorma, combine everything together and add some water if necessary. Return to the heat and cook for 5 minutes to heat through. Taste and adjust the seasoning – it should be quite spicy but may need a little more salt. Transfer to a serving dish.

9 For the garnish, heat the ghee over a medium-high heat, then add the dried onions and fry for 30–60 seconds. Transfer the onions to a piece of kitchen paper, leaving behind the ghee. Pour half of the ghee and half of the fried onions over the haleem.

10 Place all the remaining garnish ingredients and the remaining onions in a dish that has separate sections or in several small serving bowls. Put the remaining melted ghee in a jug or pitcher. Diners should help themselves and garnish their haleem as they choose.

MASALA LAMB CHAAMP
SPICED LAMB CHOPS

It is very important to choose good-quality meat, especially when cooking chops, as they should be very tender. If it is available, then spring lamb is best, although this is not such a common option in Pakistan. Mixing the meat with pulped raw papaya helps to further tenderize the meat, as the enzyme papain contained within the fruit starts to break down the fibres while the meat is marinating. The chops are delicious served on a sizzling platter with tomatoes, onions and other vegetables of your choice.

SERVES 4

8 lamb chops
2 medium onions, peeled and diced
60ml/4 tbsp vegetable oil
45ml/3 tbsp whole natural (plain) yogurt
7.5ml/1½ tsp garam masala
7.5ml/1½ tsp ground coriander
2 fresh green chillies, chopped
15ml/1 tbsp ground almonds
7.5ml/1½ tsp ginger pulp
7.5ml/1½ tsp garlic pulp
5ml/1 tsp salt
5ml/1 tsp chilli powder
45ml/3 tbsp pulped papaya
raita, naan and a daal or vegetable curry of your choice (if serving as part of a main course)

TO GARNISH

1 lemon, sliced
15ml/1 tbsp chopped fresh coriander (cilantro)
2 medium tomatoes, sliced

1 Prepare the chops by trimming as much fat as possible from them. Set aside. Purée the onions in a food processor.

2 Heat half the oil in a large pan over a medium heat, add the onion purée and fry for about 10 minutes, until golden brown. Remove the pan from heat and leave to cool.

3 Meanwhile, in a large bowl, mix together the yogurt, garam masala, ground coriander, fresh green chillies, ground almonds, ginger, garlic and salt along with the chilli powder, pulped papaya and the cooled fried onion purée.

4 Add the chops and mix everything together. Cover and place in the refrigerator to marinate for at least 4–6 hours, or ideally overnight.

5 Heat the remaining oil over a medium-high heat in a frying pan. Add the chops two at a time and fry them for 3–4 minutes per side, or until they are cooked to your preference.

6 Serve garnished with lemon slices, fresh coriander and sliced tomatoes, and serve on their own as an appetizer or as part of a main course with raita, naan, and a daal or vegetable curry of your choice.

MUTTON CHAPLEE KEBAB
CHAPLEE KEBABS

Originally a speciality of Peshawar, chaplee kebabs are now popular in all the provinces of Pakistan. The prevalent ingredient in this recipe is powdered pomegranate seeds (anardana), which gives the kebab a distinct tangy flavour, so it is worth tracking down in an Asian supermarket. Use the leanest, most finely ground mutton meat you can acquire for this.

SERVES 4

450g/1lb/2 cups minced (ground) mutton
6 spring onions (scallions), finely chopped
2 medium tomatoes, chopped
2 fresh green chillies, chopped
2.5ml/½ tsp crushed dried red chillies
6–8 black peppercorns, crushed
5ml/1 tsp coriander seeds, crushed
5ml/1 tsp white cumin seeds, crushed
5ml/1 tsp ginger pulp
5ml/1 tsp garlic pulp
5ml/1 tsp salt
7.5ml/1½ tsp powdered pomegranate seeds (anardana)
15ml/1 tbsp plain (all-purpose) flour
1 egg, whisked
vegetable oil, for shallow-frying
mint leaves and lemon wedges, to garnish
soft buns and salad, to serve (optional)

1 Place the minced mutton in a large bowl. Add all of the remaining ingredients except the oil, and mix using a spoon or your hands until everything is very well combined.

2 Break off 12 pieces of the mixture, each about the size of a golf ball. Roll them into balls, then flatten them in the palms of your hands. Slightly dampen your hands if the mixture is sticking. Place the patties on a plate.

3 Heat the oil in a large frying pan over a medium heat. Add several of the patties and fry for 3–4 minutes per side, pressing down with the back of a spatula to achieve even cooking. Transfer to a plate lined with kitchen paper and repeat until all of the kebabs are cooked.

4 Serve the kebabs garnished with mint leaves and lemon wedges. You can also serve them as a 'kebab bun' in soft buns with salad.

MASALAYDHAR QEEMA KAY KEBAB
SIMPLE MINCED MUTTON KEBABS

Kebabs are particularly popular throughout Pakistan, at mealtimes and as a snack at teatime, and they are made in a variety of ways. This particular recipe uses bread slices that are soaked in water and squeezed to remove excess moisture, which helps to bind together the mildly spiced meat mixture, as well as bulking them out and making the meat stretch further.

SERVES 4

15ml/1 tbsp vegetable oil
2 medium onions, peeled and finely diced
1 slice of white bread
450g/1lb/2 cups minced (ground) mutton
1 egg, beaten
5ml/1 tsp ginger pulp
5ml/1 tsp garlic pulp
7.5ml/1½ tsp chilli powder
7.5ml/1½ tsp garam masala
5ml/1 tsp ground cumin
1.5ml/¼ tsp ground cardamom
1.5ml/¼ tsp ground cloves
5ml/1 tsp salt
15ml/1 tbsp pulped papaya
vegetable oil, for shallow-frying

TO GARNISH
a few mint leaves
1 red onion, peeled and sliced
4–6 lemon slices

1 Heat the oil in a frying pan over a medium heat, add the onion and cook for 10–15 minutes, until softened. Leave to cool.

2 Meanwhile, soak the bread in a bowl of water for 30 seconds, then lift it out and squeeze out the excess moisture.

3 Mix together the minced mutton, squeezed bread, egg, ginger, garlic, chilli powder, garam masala, ground cumin, cardamom and cloves, salt and the fried onions, until everything is well combined.

4 Add the pulped papaya and stir to combine thoroughly. Cover and leave to marinate in the refrigerator for about 1 hour.

5 Break off 12 pieces of the mixture, each about the size of a golf ball, roll them into balls, then flatten them in the palms of your hands and place them on a plate. Slightly dampen your hands if the mixture is sticking.

6 Heat the oil in a frying pan over a medium heat, then add some of the kebabs and fry until for 3–4 minutes on each side, until they are cooked on both sides. Remove to a plate lined with kitchen paper and repeat the cooking process with the remaining kebabs.

7 Once all the kebabs are ready, place them on a serving dish and garnish with the mint leaves, sliced red onions and lemon slices.

MUTTON SEEKH KEBAB

TRADITIONAL SEEKH KEBABS

These kebabs are usually bought from roadside cafés or restaurants, where the thick spears around which the meat is pressed can be seen neatly lined up over a bed of blisteringly hot coals. The traditional skewers are quite thick, which means that the hole left in the middle of the cooked kebab is big enough for you to look through. This makes them very light in texture. However, these skewers are not widely available outside Asia, so use standard metal skewers and try to make the layer of meat as thin as possible. Ask your butcher to give you mince from the leg of lamb and to put it through the mincing machine at least twice so it has a very fine texture.

SERVES 4

1 medium onion, peeled and roughly chopped
2 fresh green chillies
15ml/1 tbsp chopped fresh coriander (cilantro)
5ml/1 tsp ginger pulp
5ml/1 tsp garlic pulp
5ml/1 tsp chilli powder
5ml/1 tsp salt
1.5ml/¼ tsp ground turmeric
2.5ml/½ tsp ground allspice
2.5ml/½ tsp ground mace
450g/1lb/2 cups very finely minced (ground) mutton leg
15ml/1 tbsp pulped papaya
vegetable oil, for basting

TO SERVE

1 onion, peeled and sliced into rings
shredded iceberg lettuce
2 tomatoes, sliced
½ cucumber, peeled and sliced
about 4 naan
60ml/4 tbsp raita
1 lemon, cut into wedges

1 Blend together the chopped onion, fresh green chillies and chopped fresh coriander in a food processor.

2 Transfer to a large bowl and add all the spices and the minced mutton. Mix everything together with a spoon or using your hands until thoroughly combined. Stir in the pulped papaya, then cover and leave for about 1 hour in the refrigerator.

3 Preheat a grill or broiler to high. Start by breaking off 12 balls of the mince, each a little bigger than a golf ball. Using dampened hands, shape each ball into thin kebabs about 13cm/5in long. If you are using metal skewers, form the kebabs around these, pressing the meat so it sticks to the skewer and stays together.

4 Place the kebabs, on or off skewers, on a grill rack and cook under the hot grill for 7–10 minutes, turning around frequently and basting the meat with a little oil, until all sides are cooked through and sizzling.

5 To serve, make a salad from the onion rings, lettuce, tomatoes and cucumber. Allow two or three kebabs per person, and serve with the salad, naan, raita and lemon wedges for squeezing over. Allow diners to assemble their own rolls.

VARIATION To shallow-fry the kebabs, cook them in a little oil in a frying pan over a medium heat for 3–4 minutes per side, turning them around gently until they are cooked through.

SEEKH KEBAB ROLLS
MASALA MINCED MUTTON KEBAB ROLLS

Kebabs are a very popular snack – not surprisingly given that they are extremely tasty – but they are also substantial enough to be a main meal when served as rolls. These ones consist of tender, juicy little patties garnished with tomato, onions, mint-flavoured yogurt, raita and masala tomato sauce, all wrapped up in a naan, chapati or paratha. The patties are traditionally cooked over glowing coals on thick metal skewers, but here they are shallow-fried so they can be made in the kitchen as well as outdoors on a barbecue.

1 Place the minced mutton in a large bowl along with the soaked bread slices and mix these together thoroughly.

2 Add the ginger, garlic, chilli powder, garam masala, ground allspice, ground cinnamon and salt and mix well.

3 Place the onion, fresh green chillies, fresh coriander and mint leaves in a food processor and blend for about 1 minute, until finely chopped. Add the mixture to the mince along with the beaten egg and blend everything together using a spoon or your hands.

4 Form the mixture into 8–10 kebabs, each about 7.5cm/3in long, and place them on a dish.

5 When all the kebabs are made, heat the oil in a frying pan over a medium heat and fry in batches for about 3–4 minutes on each side, until they are cooked through. Transfer to a plate lined with kitchen paper and keep warm.

6 Once all the kebabs are cooked, assemble the rolls. Spread about 15ml/1 tbsp each of raita and masala sauce (or any sauce of your choice) over each chapati or naan. Add a kebab and then top with diced tomato and onion rings. Roll over the bread to encase the filling and serve the rolls immediately, with lemon wedges for squeezing over.

SERVES 4–5

500g/1¼lb/2½ cups minced (ground) mutton
2 slices of white bread, soaked in water for 1 minute, then squeezed
5ml/1 tsp ginger pulp
5ml/1 tsp garlic pulp
10ml/2 tsp chilli powder
7.5ml/1½ tsp garam masala
5ml/1 tsp ground allspice
2.5ml/½ tsp ground cinnamon
7.5ml/1½ tsp salt
1 medium onion, peeled and roughly chopped
2 fresh green chillies
15ml/1 tbsp chopped fresh coriander (cilantro)
2–3 mint leaves
1 egg, beaten
vegetable oil, for shallow-frying

TO SERVE

120–180ml/8–12 tbsp raita
120–180ml/8–12 tbsp masala sauce (or any sauce of your choice)
8–12 chapatis or naan
4–6 tomatoes, diced
2 onions, peeled and sliced into rings
2 lemons, cut into wedges

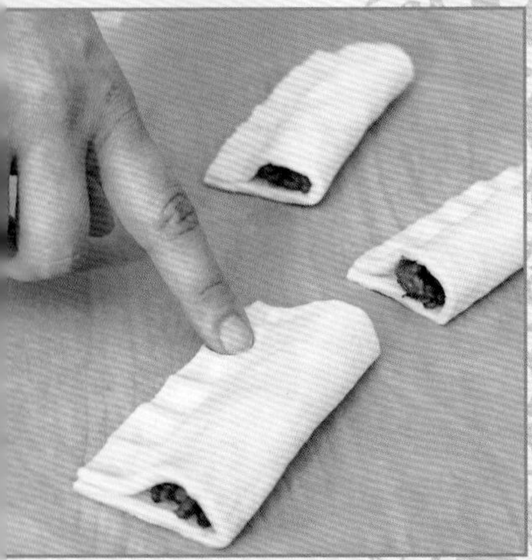

QEEMA PATTIES
MINCED LAMB PATTIES IN PUFF PASTRY

These patties, as they are known in Pakistan, are made from spicy lamb cooked with onions, green chillies and fresh coriander encased in golden, fluffy puff pastry. Pastry is a hangover from the days of the Raj, when the British introduced this and many other Western ingredients and recipes to the Indian subcontinent. This particular hybrid treat remains a great favourite on Sunday afternoons, when it is served with tea. Often bought warm from the oven in bakeries in larger towns and cities in Pakistan, they are simple to make at home if you buy chilled ready-made puff pastry.

SERVES 3–4

- 60ml/4 tbsp vegetable oil
- 4 curry leaves
- 2 medium onions, peeled and diced
- 5ml/1 tsp ginger pulp
- 5ml/1 tsp garlic pulp
- 7.5ml/1½ tsp chilli powder
- 1.5ml/¼ tsp ground turmeric
- 5ml/1 tsp salt, or to taste
- 30ml/2 tbsp chopped fresh coriander (cilantro)
- 2 fresh green chillies, chopped (seeded if preferred)
- 500g/1¼lb/2¼ cups lean minced (ground) lamb
- 500g/1¼lb all-butter puff pastry
- a sauce or chutney of your choice, such as masala or tamarind sauce, green chutney or tomato ketchup, to serve

1 Heat the oil in a large frying pan over a medium heat. Add the curry leaves and onions and fry for 10–15 minutes, until the onion is soft and golden brown. Add the ginger, garlic, chilli powder, ground turmeric, salt, half of the fresh coriander and half the chopped chilli.

2 Stir in the minced lamb and leave to cook for 7–10 minutes, stirring occasionally.

3 Increase the heat slightly and stir-fry the lamb, breaking up any balls that may have formed, for about 10 minutes, until the lamb is darker in colour. Stir in the remaining coriander and chilli and transfer the mixture to a dish. Set aside and leave to cool.

4 Preheat the oven to 180°C/350°F/Gas 4. Roll out the puff pastry to a square measuring 39 x 39cm/15 x 15in, then divide this into 9 squares each measuring 13 x 13cm/5 x 5in.

5 Place about 10ml/2 tsp of the lamb mixture on each square and fold over to make about a 13cm/5in-long patty.

6 Brush the edges with water and pinch them together firmly, then brush the outside of the pastry with beaten egg. Continue to do this until you have made 9 patties.

7 Place the patties on a greased baking dish, leaving at least 2.5cm/1in between them to allow for spreading.

8 Bake in the preheated oven for about 20 minutes, or until the pastry is cooked and golden. Serve with the sauce or chutney of your choice.

BOTI TIKKA
MARINATED GRILLED LAMB

I have fond memories of eating delectable boti tikkas served on a sizzling dish during my childhood in Karachi, where cooking food on a barbecue is especially popular. There is always a buzz around the numerous and excellent restaurants dedicated to the cooking technique, all of which tend to be very busy. The moderate weather of the city and its mild and pleasant evenings make it particularly conducive to dining out, particularly al fresco, and one is very easily drawn to the barbecue restaurants because of their mouthwatering aromas. Boti means off-the-bone meat cut into fairly small cubes. Make sure the meat is very lean and cut into 5cm/2in cubes.

SERVES 4

450g/1lb lamb or goat shoulder or leg meat
60ml/4 tbsp pulped papaya
4 fresh green chillies, roughly chopped
30ml/2 tbsp chopped fresh coriander (cilantro)
15ml/1 tbsp ginger pulp
7.5ml/1½ tsp garlic pulp
10ml/2 tsp garam masala
7.5ml/1½ tsp ground cumin
7.5ml/1½ tsp ground coriander
7.5ml/1½ tsp salt
1.5ml/¼ tsp ground mace
1.5ml/¼ tsp freshly grated nutmeg
10ml/2 tsp chilli powder
2.5ml/½ tsp ground allspice
2.5ml/½ tsp ground turmeric
60–90ml/4–6 tbsp lemon juice
45ml/3 tbsp whole natural (plain) yogurt
vegetable oil, to baste
raita and naan, to serve

TO GARNISH

1 medium onion, peeled and cut into rings
2–3 fresh green chillies, split lengthwise
2 tomatoes, sliced
15ml/1 tbsp chopped fresh coriander (cilantro)
2 lemons, cut into wedges

1 Prepare the meat by removing all the fat, then cut it into 5cm/2in cubes and place it in a large bowl.

2 Blend together the pulped papaya, fresh green chillies, fresh coriander, ginger and garlic in a blender or food processor. Add this to the meat, stir to combine, then cover and set aside at room temperature for 2 hours.

3 Meanwhile, blend together the garam masala, ground cumin and coriander, salt, ground mace, nutmeg, chilli powder, ground allspice and turmeric, lemon juice and yogurt in a separate bowl.

4 Add the yogurt mixture to the bowl containing the meat, stir to combine everything well, re-cover and leave to marinate for 4–6 hours.

5 When you are ready to cook, preheat the grill or broiler to high, or prepare a barbecue so that the coals are glowing red and are coated in a fine white ash. Lightly oil the bars of the grill rack.

6 Thread the lamb pieces on to long metal skewers. Place the skewers under the grill or on the barbecue and cook for about 10–15 minutes, until cooked though and lightly charred, turning the skewers around occasionally and basting them with oil.

7 Garnish with onion rings, fresh chillies, tomatoes, fresh coriander and lemons and serve with raita and naan.

VARIATION Boti tikka can be made using beef, goat or lamb, but lamb is the easiest to tenderize. If you do decide to use beef, allow it to marinate overnight.

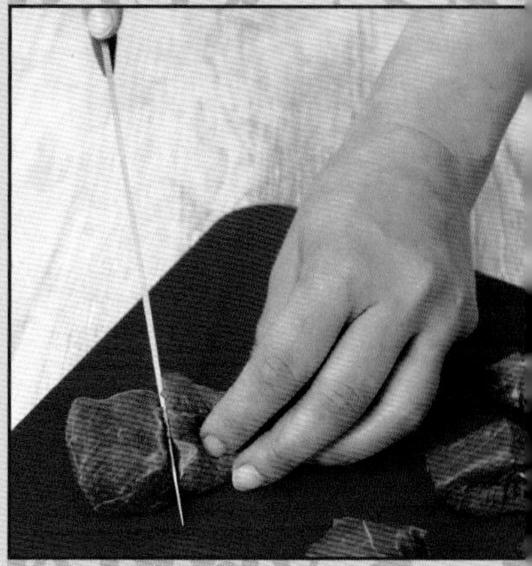

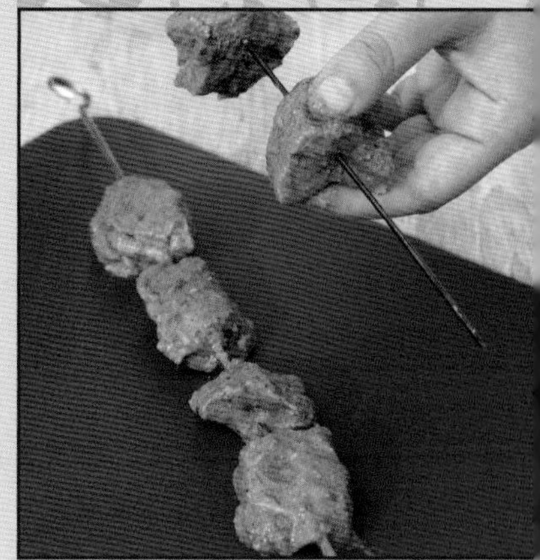

MUTTON DUM KA QEEMA

GRILLED MINCED MUTTON

This classic way of cooking minced mutton is sometimes referred to as dum kay kebab and originated in the south of India. Traditionally, hot coals would be placed directly on the surface of the meat once it had been put in a heatproof dish, then it would be covered with a lid and allowed to char. At home, you can replicate this to some extent using a very hot grill to sear the surface of the meat paste and give the dish its trademark smoky flavour.

SERVES 4

60–75ml/4–5 tbsp vegetable oil
2 medium onions, peeled and chopped
500g/1¼lb/2¼ cups minced (ground) mutton
30ml/2 tbsp whole natural (plain) yogurt
5ml/1 tsp garam masala
7.5ml/1½ tsp ground coriander
5ml/1 tsp ground cumin
1.5ml/¼ tsp ground allspice
5ml/1 tsp ginger pulp
7.5ml/1½ tsp garlic pulp
5–7.5ml/1–1½ tsp chilli powder
5ml/1 tsp salt, or to taste
30ml/2 tbsp chopped fresh coriander (cilantro)
2 fresh green chillies, roughly chopped (seeded if preferred)

TO GARNISH

1 onion, peeled and sliced into rings
4 lemon wedges
2 each fresh red and green chillies
15ml/1 tbsp chopped fresh coriander (cilantro)

1 Heat the oil in a large pan over a medium heat, add the onions and fry for 10–15 minutes, until soft and golden brown.

2 Meanwhile, put the mutton, yogurt, garam masala, ground coriander, cumin and allspice, ginger, garlic, chilli powder and salt in a food processor and process for about 1 minute, until well combined.

3 Add the fresh coriander and fresh green chillies and process again for another 1 minute.

4 Transfer the meat mixture to the pan with the onions and cook for 5–7 minutes, until cooked through, stirring frequently to prevent it from sticking.

5 Remove the pan from the heat and let the mixture cool down. Process the cooled mixture in a food processor for 1–2 minutes, until smooth. Preheat a grill or broiler to high.

6 Transfer the meat to a heatproof dish and place this under the hot grill for about 5 minutes, keeping a close eye on it and turning it around to ensure even cooking. Let the meat char a little on top.

7 Remove the dish from under the heat when this is achieved. Serve garnished with the onion rings, lemon wedges, fresh chillies and chopped fresh coriander.

ALOO AUR MUTTON KAY CUTLETS
POTATO AND MUTTON CUTLETS

Unlike their Western counterparts (slices of deep-fried breadcrumb-coated meat, chicken or fish), cutlets in Pakistan and elsewhere in the subcontinent are made from a combination of soft mashed potato and a lightly spiced meat or chicken mixture that is dipped in egg and breadcrumbs and shallow-fried. In this incarnation, the mutton element is a mild one (at least by Pakistani standards), spiced only with some black pepper, salt and a few fresh red chillies.

SERVES 4

5 medium potatoes, peeled and chopped
7.5ml/1½ tsp salt
30ml/2 tbsp finely chopped fresh coriander (cilantro)
75ml/5 tbsp vegetable oil
1 medium onion, peeled and chopped
5ml/1 tsp ginger pulp
5ml/1 tsp garlic pulp
7.5ml/1½ tsp coarsely ground black pepper
500g/1¼lb/2¼ cups minced (ground) mutton
2 fresh red chillies, sliced
2 eggs, beaten
50g/2oz/1 cup fresh white breadcrumbs
vegetable oil, for shallow-frying

1 Boil the potatoes in a large pan of boiling water for 10–15 minutes, until soft. Drain, then mash the potatoes. Add the salt and half of the finely chopped coriander and set aside.

2 Heat the oil in a pan over a medium heat, add the onion and fry for 10–15 minutes, until soft and golden brown.

3 Add the ginger, garlic and black pepper followed by the minced mutton and stir-fry for 10–15 minutes. Mash any lumps that form in the mince using a spatula, so the mixture is quite smooth.

4 Add the sliced red chillies and the remaining fresh coriander and stir-fry for a further 5–7 minutes, until the mixture is quite dry. Remove from the heat and leave to cool.

5 Break off 12 balls of cooled mashed potatoes, each a little bigger than a golf ball, and pat them flat in the palm of your hand.

6 Make a slight dip in the middle of each, into which you can place about 15ml/1 tbsp of the minced meat mixture. Fold over the potato to make a patty.

7 Put the egg in one shallow dish and the breadcrumbs in another. Dip each patty first in the beaten egg and then in the breadcrumbs.

8 Heat the oil for shallow-frying in a large frying pan over a medium heat. Fry the patties in batches for about 3–4 minutes per side, until they are golden brown all over, taking care not to let them burn.

9 Transfer to a plate lined with kitchen paper while you repeat the process to cook all of the patties. Serve hot on their own as a snack, or as part of a meal with other dishes.

PESHAWARI MUTTON KADAHI

AROMATIC MUTTON STEW

Rich in both flavour and colour, this fragrant stew of tender mutton is more piquant than dishes from some other regions, a spiciness that is balanced by the addition of a little sweetness from the sugar and the zingy freshness brought by the slices of raw fresh ginger used as a garnish.

SERVES 4

- 2 medium onions, peeled and halved
- 90ml/6 tbsp vegetable oil
- 2.5ml/½ tsp soft light brown sugar
- 10ml/2 tsp ginger pulp
- 7.5ml/1½ tsp garlic pulp
- 10ml/2 tsp ground coriander
- 7.5ml/1½ tsp ground cumin
- 7.5ml/1½ tsp chilli powder
- 500g/1¼lb mutton on the bone, cut into small pieces (you can ask your butcher to do this for you, if you like)
- 4–6 black peppercorns
- 1 small cinnamon stick
- 2 black cardamoms
- 5 medium tomatoes, sliced
- 7.5ml/1½ tsp salt
- 30ml/2 tbsp whole natural (plain) yogurt, whisked
- 475ml/16fl oz/2 cups water
- 2 each fresh green and red chillies
- 15ml/1 tbsp chopped fresh coriander (cilantro)
- 8–10 slices fresh root ginger, to garnish
- 1.5ml/¼ tsp garam masala
- naan, to serve

1 Process the onions in a food processor to form a pulp.

2 Heat 45ml/3 tbsp of the oil in a large pan, add the onion pulp and fry for about 10 minutes, until golden brown. Transfer the onion to a bowl and set aside.

3 In a bowl, mix together the soft light brown sugar, ginger, garlic, ground coriander and cumin, and the chilli powder.

4 Place the lamb in the pan in which the onions were fried, along with the remaining oil. Add the peppercorns, cinnamon and cardamoms and fry for 5–7 minutes, until the meat is sealed.

5 Add the sliced tomatoes and the ground spice mixture to the pan and stir to combine thoroughly. Add the salt and whisked yogurt, then pour in the water. Stir to combine well, then cover and cook for 20–25 minutes, stirring and checking it occasionally.

6 Once the mutton is tender, taste and adjust the seasoning as necessary. Remove the lid and stir-fry for about 10 minutes, until oil begins to appear around the sides of the pan.

7 Add half the fresh green and red chillies and half the chopped fresh coriander and stir to combine.

8 Transfer to a serving dish and serve garnished with the remaining chillies and fresh coriander, and the ginger slices. Finally, sprinkle over the garam masala and serve with naan.

NEHARI

LAMB NEHARI

Regarded as the national dish of Pakistan, nehari is known for its piquancy and texture. The name has its origins in Arabic and means 'day' or 'morning' and it was typically served to kings and nobility around sunrise, after the Muslim early morning Fajr prayer. The Mughals brought it to the Indian subcontinent and it soon became a nationwide tradition among the Muslims. The dish comprises slow-cooked large, tender shanks or pieces of beef, mutton or lamb and, while not completely authentic, even chicken. Known for its spiciness, it is a delicious curry with a thick, flavoursome sauce that is often sold with naan fresh from the tandoor in specialist restaurants and roadside cafes early in the morning, particularly on weekends.

SERVES 4

2 medium onions, peeled and halved
120ml/4fl oz/½ cup vegetable oil
2 bay leaves
900g/2lb leg of lamb on the bone, cut into 7.5–10cm/3–4in cubes, or 3–4 medium lamb shanks
15ml/1 tbsp garam masala
15ml/1 tbsp ground coriander
10ml/2 tsp garlic pulp
10ml/2 tsp ginger pulp
5ml/1 tsp freshly grated nutmeg
10ml/2 tsp ground fennel seeds
10ml/2 tsp paprika
30ml/2 tbsp tomato paste
7.5ml/1½ tsp salt
1 litre/1¾ pints/4 cups water, plus 60ml/4 tbsp to make a flour paste
30ml/2 tbsp plain (all-purpose) flour
15ml/1 tbsp chopped fresh coriander (cilantro)
2 lemons, cut into wedges, to serve
naan or parathas, to serve

TO GARNISH

4–6 fresh green chillies, chopped
45ml/3 tbsp chopped fresh coriander (cilantro)
45ml/3 tbsp peeled and finely sliced fresh root ginger

1 Process the onions in a food processor to form a pulp.

2 Heat 60ml/4 tbsp of the oil in a very large pan over a medium heat and fry the bay leaves for about 30 seconds. Add the meat, followed by the garam masala. Fry for about 5 minutes, to seal the meat.

3 Add the ground coriander, garlic, ginger, nutmeg, ground fennel seeds, paprika and tomato paste and stir to combine. Add the salt and stir once more, then remove from the heat.

4 In a separate pan, heat the remaining oil over a medium heat, add the pulped onion and fry for about 10 minutes, until golden brown.

5 Add the onion pulp to the lamb and combine everything together. Pour in the water, return to the heat and bring to the boil.

6 Reduce the heat to low and cook for 45–60 minutes, checking occasionally and stirring. The curry is ready once the liquid has reduced by at least half and the meat is tender and falling off the bone.

7 Dissolve the flour in the 60ml/4 tbsp water, whisking it well to make a smooth paste. Pour this over the lamb while slowly and gently stirring the curry. Cook for a further 7–10 minutes, stirring frequently, until the sauce is thick.

8 Using a ladle, transfer the curry to a serving dish, or individual deep plates if using shanks – allowing one per person. Serve garnished with chillies, fresh coriander, and ginger, and accompany with lemon wedges, and naan or parathas.

THALI HUWI KALEJI

FRIED MUTTON LIVER

This is a special favourite dish served at the festival of Eid al-Adha, made with extremely fresh liver taken from sacrificial lambs. The liver is cut into cubes and, after a thorough washing, covered in turmeric to suppress the inherent smell. The liver cubes are then fried in a pan with various aromatic spices, before being served with fresh parathas.

1 Rub the ground turmeric into the cubed liver and set aside.

2 Put the onion, fresh green chillies and fresh coriander in a food processor and blend for about 2 minutes, until very finely chopped.

3 Rub the onion mixture on to the liver along with the salt, chilli powder, ground cumin, ginger, garlic, ground allspice and malt vinegar. Cover and set aside in the refrigerator for about 1 hour.

4 When you are ready to cook, heat the oil in a wok or heavy frying pan (or a kadahi if you have one) over a low-medium heat. Add the liver mixture and fry it for 8–10 minutes, moving it around, until the water is absorbed and the liver is only just cooked through.

5 Transfer to a serving dish and serve garnished with onion rings, fresh green chillies, sprigs of fresh coriander and lemon wedges.

SERVES 4

2.5ml/½ tsp ground turmeric
500g/1¼lb mutton liver, cut into cubes
2 medium onions, peeled and chopped
3 chopped fresh green chillies
30ml/2 tbsp chopped fresh coriander (cilantro)
7.5ml/1½ tsp salt
10ml/2 tsp chilli powder
10ml/2 tsp ground cumin
7.5ml/1½ tsp ginger pulp
7.5ml/1½ tsp garlic pulp
2.5ml/½ tsp ground allspice
60–90ml/4–6 tbsp malt vinegar
120–150ml/4fl oz–¼ pint/½–⅔ cup vegetable oil

TO GARNISH

1 onion, peeled and cut into rings
4–6 fresh green chillies, split lengthwise
sprigs of fresh coriander (cilantro)
6–8 lemon wedges

GAYE KAY GOSHTH KAY GOLA KEBAB

BEEF GOLA KEBABS

These spicy beef kebabs include the unusual addition of crushed cornflakes, a non-traditional ingredient that I find lends bulk and a little texture to the tasty strips of seasoned meat. They are especially delicious served sizzling hot with a mint chutney and naan. These can either be cooked on a barbecue or just shallow-fried in a pan, as here. As with lamb in Pakistan, beef is generally bought from a market or butchers rather than a supermarket, as cooks prefer to specify the cut and preparation of the chosen product to ensure it meets their exacting standards.

SERVES 4

30ml/2 tbsp vegetable oil, plus extra for shallow-frying
1 medium onion, peeled and diced
500g/1¼lb/2¼ cups minced (ground) beef
7.5ml/1½ tsp ginger pulp
5ml/1 tsp garlic pulp
5ml/1 tsp crushed dried red chillies
5ml/1 tsp ground cumin
5ml/1 tsp ground coriander
1.5ml/¼ tsp ground black pepper
2.5ml/½ tsp garam masala
5ml/1 tsp salt
15ml/1 tbsp pulped papaya
30ml/2 tbsp cornflakes
1 fresh green chilli
4–6 fresh mint leaves
15ml/1 tbsp chopped fresh coriander (cilantro)
raita, chutney and naan, to serve

1 Heat the oil in a frying pan over a medium heat, add the onion and cook for 10–15 minutes, until soft and golden brown.

2 Remove the onion using a slotted spoon, draining as much oil as possible, and place it in a food processor. Add the minced beef, ginger, garlic, crushed dried red chillies, ground cumin, coriander and black pepper, garam masala, salt and papaya pulp and process together for about 1 minute. Transfer to a large bowl and set aside.

3 Rinse out and dry the food processor, then add the cornflakes and process until they form a powder. Add to the beef mixture in the bowl.

4 Put the fresh green chilli, mint leaves and fresh coriander in the food processor and process for about 1 minute, until finely chopped. Add to the beef and blend everything together using a spoon or your hands.

6 With damp hands, break off 12 small balls of the beef mixture and form them into sausage shapes measuring about 5cm/2in. Place these on a plate.

7 Heat the oil for shallow-frying in a large frying pan and cook the kebabs in batches for about 3–4 minutes on each side, gently turning them occasionally, until cooked through.

8 Serve with raita, a chutney of your choice, and some naan.

GAYE KAY GOSHTH KAY SHAAMI KEBAB

SPICED BEEF PATTIES

There is a variety of different shaami kebabs, which can be made with lamb, beef, mutton or even chicken, and they can also be prepared in several ways. Some are made using meat that is cooked, ground in a food processor, then combined with lentils to bind; others comprise just meat. The ones here are the former type, and are shaped into small flat round shapes that are then shallow-fried. They make an excellent accompaniment to any meal and are very popular at dinner parties. They freeze well and are a good back-up for a quick lunch, served on toast or with chapati or naan, with a salad and any sauce of your choice. Here, I have used beef mince but you may substitute any other meat if you prefer.

SERVES 4–5

- 500g/1¼lb/2¼ cups lean minced (ground) beef
- 115g/4oz/½ cup chana daal
- 1½ medium onions, peeled and chopped
- 4 dried red chillies
- 7.5ml/1½ tsp cumin seeds
- 7.5ml/1½ tsp coriander seeds
- 6 black peppercorns
- 7.5ml/1½ tsp cardamom seeds
- 5ml/1 tsp ginger pulp
- 5ml/1 tsp garlic pulp
- 7.5ml/1½ tsp salt
- 2.5ml/½ tsp ground allspice
- 30ml/2 tbsp chopped fresh coriander (cilantro)
- 475ml/16fl oz/2 cups water
- 1 fresh green chilli
- 15ml/1 tbsp fresh mint
- 1 egg, beaten
- vegetable oil, for shallow-frying
- naan, raita and daal, to serve

1 Put the minced beef in a large pan. Add the chana daal, 1 chopped onion, the dried red chillies, cumin seeds, coriander seeds, peppercorns, cardamom seeds, ginger, garlic, salt and ground allspice and mix everything together.

2 Add half of the fresh coriander and the water and cook over a medium heat for 20–25 minutes or until the liquid has evaporated fully. Remove from the heat and set aside.

3 Meanwhile, process the remaining fresh coriander, fresh green chilli, fresh mint and remaining ½ onion in a blender for about 30 seconds. Add the egg and the minced beef mixture and process until it is quite pasty. Transfer to a bowl.

4 Break off 12–15 lumps of meat, each a little bigger than a golf ball. Using the palm and fingers of your hands, pat these balls flat to make patties about 1cm/½in thick.

5 Heat the oil in a large frying pan over a medium-high heat and cook the patties in batches for about 3–4 minutes per side, turning them gently, until they are cooked through.

6 Serve hot, accompanied by naan, raita and a daal.

VEGETABLES & DAALS

RECIPES

PAKISTANI OMELETTE
SPICY PAKISTANI-STYLE OMELETTE

MASALA ALOO AUR BAINGUN
MASALA POTATOES AND AUBERGINES

KHATAY MEETHAY ALOO KADI PATTA
POTATO CURRY WITH CURRY LEAVES

THALI HUWI PHOOL GOBI
FRIED CAULIFLOWER

CHANA PALAK
CHICKPEAS AND SPINACH

BHINDI TAMATAR
OKRA WITH TOMATOES

TARKA DAAL
CLASSIC TARKA DAAL

MAASH KI DAAL
SPICED URID TARKA DAAL

DAAL MAKHANI
CREAMY BLACK LENTIL DAAL

PAKISTANI OMELETTE
SPICY PAKISTANI-STYLE OMELETTE

All top hotels in Pakistan serve a lavish weekend brunch spread, and the tradition has caught on in many sophisticated homes too. Of the many dishes on offer, one of the most popular is a well-made Pakistani omelette. Simple yet delicious, it is usually served with toast or paratha and some mango chutney.

1 Combine the onion, fresh coriander, fresh green chillies and tomato (if using) in a large bowl.

2 Add the eggs and whisk until the mixture becomes frothy. Add the salt and bicarbonate of soda and whisk again.

3 Heat a little oil in a frying pan and pour in half the mixture. Swirl it round to coat the pan, then fry the omelette over a medium heat for 2 minutes. Gently turn it over and cook until it is fully cooked through, pressing on the top.

4 Transfer to a serving plate and cook the remaining mixture in the same way.

5 Serve immediately, with paratha and some mango chutney.

SERVES 2

1 small onion, peeled and very finely diced
30ml/2 tbsp finely chopped fresh coriander (cilantro)
2–3 fresh green chillies, seeded if liked and finely chopped
1 tomato, diced (optional)
3 large (US extra large) eggs
1.5ml/¼ tsp salt
a large pinch of bicarbonate of soda (baking soda)
vegetable oil, for shallow-frying
paratha and mango chutney, to serve

MASALA ALOO AUR BAINGUN
MASALA POTATOES AND AUBERGINES

Potatoes, being a starchy carbohydrate, almost always make good side dishes, whatever their incarnation. This one is especially nutritionally beneficial, containing protein in the form of chickpeas alongside small, tender aubergines to create a sustaining meal-in-a-bowl. As with many vegetarian dishes, it is also extremely economical and since the vast majority of the ingredients are kitchen staples, it is easy to throw together at a moment's notice.

SERVES 4

60ml/4 tbsp vegetable oil
4–6 curry leaves
1.5ml/¼ tsp onion seeds
2–3 dried red chillies
1.5ml/¼ tsp cumin seeds
1.5ml/¼ tsp ground fennel seeds
5ml/1 tsp garlic pulp
5ml/1 tsp ginger pulp
5ml/1 tsp ground coriander
5ml/1 tsp ground cumin
2.5ml/½ tsp ground turmeric
2 medium onions, peeled and diced
3 small aubergines (eggplants), cut into cubes
5 small new potatoes, peeled and sliced
200g/7oz canned chickpeas, drained
250ml/8fl oz/1 cup water
30ml/2 tbsp lemon juice
½ each red and green (bell) peppers, seeded and roughly diced
15ml/1 tbsp tamarind sauce
5ml/1 tsp chopped fresh coriander (cilantro), to garnish

1 Heat the oil in a wok or frying pan over a medium heat. Add the curry leaves, onion seeds, dried red chillies, cumin seeds, fennel seeds, garlic, ginger, and the ground coriander, cumin and turmeric. Fry for 2–3 minutes.

2 Add the onion and fry for about 5 minutes, then add the aubergine and potato. Stir-fry for a few minutes until it has all blended together and the vegetables are starting to soften, then add the chickpeas and water.

3 Cover and cook for 10–15 minutes, until the vegetables are cooked through.

4 Add the lemon juice, diced peppers and tamarind sauce, mix everything together to combine and transfer to a serving dish. Serve garnished with some fresh coriander.

KHATAY MEETHAY ALOO KADI PATTA
POTATO CURRY WITH CURRY LEAVES

Potatoes are one of Pakistan's most important crops, especially in the Punjab where growing conditions are ideal. With such a bountiful, cheap supply on tap, it is little wonder that aloo appear on so many tables, providing sustenance for everyone from the poorest labourer to the wealthiest businessman. Here, they are transformed into a satisfying sweet-and-sour curry that is excellent served with poori or chapatis and mango chutney.

1 Heat the oil in a medium wok or heavy frying pan over a medium heat. Add the onion, mustard and cumin seeds, dried red chillies and curry leaves and stir-fry for about 1 minute.

2 Add the onions and fry for 10–15 minutes, until soft and golden brown.

3 Stir in the ginger, garlic, ground turmeric, chilli powder and half the fresh coriander, followed by the salt. Stir-fry for 1 minute to blend the spices together, then add 1 finely chopped green chilli. Add the diced potato and lower the heat.

4 Pour in the tamarind sauce, lemon juice and water and stir-fry for 1 minute. Cover with a lid and cook for 10–15 minutes, until the potatoes are fully cooked.

5 Stir in the remaining green chilli and the fresh coriander. Serve with poori or chapatis and some mango chutney.

SERVES 4

- 60–90ml/4–6 tbsp vegetable oil
- 1.5ml/¼ tsp onion seeds
- 1.5ml/¼ tsp mustard seeds
- 1.5ml/¼ tsp cumin seeds
- 2–3 dried red chillies
- 8–10 curry leaves
- 2 medium onions, peeled and chopped
- 5ml/1 tsp ginger pulp
- 5ml/1 tsp garlic pulp
- 1.5ml/¼ tsp ground turmeric
- 7.5ml/1½ tsp chilli powder
- 45ml/3 tbsp chopped fresh coriander (cilantro)
- 5ml/1 tsp salt
- 2 fresh green chillies, finely chopped
- 2 large potatoes, finely diced
- 30ml/2 tbsp tamarind sauce
- 15ml/1 tbsp lemon juice
- 120ml/4fl oz/½ cup water
- poori or chapatis and mango chutney, to serve

SERVES 4

- 60ml/4 tbsp vegetable oil
- 4–5 curry leaves
- 1.5ml/¼ tsp onion seeds
- 1 large onion, peeled and diced
- 5ml/1 tsp ginger pulp
- 5ml/1 tsp crushed dried red chillies
- 2.5ml/½ tsp salt
- 1 small cauliflower, cut into pieces
- 30ml/2 tbsp chilli and garlic sauce
- 15ml/1 tbsp lemon juice
- 1 red (bell) pepper, seeded and roughly sliced
- 15ml/1 tbsp chopped fresh coriander (cilantro)

THALI HUWI PHOOL GOBI
FRIED CAULIFLOWER

The creamy curds of a fresh cauliflower are the perfect carriers for a wide range of spices, the subtle yet distinctive flavour both standing up to and enhancing the blend of spices. This quick and easy dish is most often served as an accompaniment, although it could also be an appetizer or even a main course when served with appropriate quantities of bread or rice.

1 Heat the oil in a large pan over a medium heat. Add the curry leaves, onion seeds, ginger, crushed dried red chillies and salt and stir-fry for 2–3 minutes.

2 Add the cauliflower pieces and continue to stir-fry for a further 7–10 minutes, making sure that the cauliflower remains crunchy.

3 Stir in the chilli and garlic sauce, lemon juice, pepper and fresh coriander. Transfer to a serving dish and serve.

CHANA PALAK
CHICKPEAS AND SPINACH

Spiced chickpeas in various guises are widely enjoyed throughout Pakistan, especially at breakfast time. This version is given a different touch by the addition of fresh spinach and is really worth a try. Serve it with poori or rice if eaten for lunch or dinner.

SERVES 4

2.5ml/½ tsp ginger pulp
2.5ml/½ tsp garlic pulp
2.5ml/½ tsp crushed dried chilli flakes
2.5ml/½ tsp ground coriander
2.5ml/½ tsp ground cumin
5ml/1 tsp garam masala
7.5ml/1½ tsp mango powder (amchoor)
5ml/1 tsp salt, or to taste
30ml/2 tbsp tamarind sauce
30ml/2 tbsp tomato ketchup
30–45ml/2–3 tbsp vegetable oil
1 bay leaf
1.5ml/¼ tsp white cumin seeds
200g/7oz canned chickpeas, drained
50–75g/2–3oz fresh spinach
a generous pinch of chaat masala
1 fresh green chilli, split lengthways and seeded
2.5cm/1in piece of fresh root ginger, peeled and cut into strips

1 In a mixing bowl, blend together the ginger, garlic, crushed dried chilli flakes, ground coriander and cumin, garam masala, mango powder, salt, tamarind sauce and the tomato ketchup.

2 Heat the oil in a wok or frying pan over a medium heat, then add the bay leaf and white cumin seeds. Add the spice mixture to the oil and stir-fry for 2–3 minutes.

3 Add the chickpeas and fresh spinach and keep stir-frying for 5–7 minutes, reducing the heat if necessary.

4 Transfer to a serving dish, sprinkle over some chaat masala and garnish with the split green chilli and ginger strips.

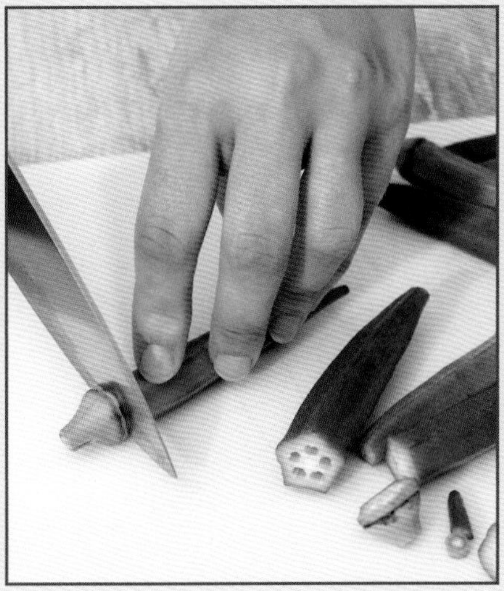

BHINDI TAMATAR
OKRA WITH TOMATOES

Okra are extremely popular in Pakistan, the slender, dusty-green 'fingers' being a common sight at most markets. They have a slightly bitter flavour that is wonderfully offset in this vegetarian dish by the sweetness of the tomato and sugar and the warming blend of spices. Simple and quick to prepare, bhindi tamatar makes a tasty meal when served with freshly made chapatis and daal.

SERVES 4

275g/10oz okra
60–75ml/4–5 tbsp vegetable oil
30ml/2 tbsp tomato paste
5ml/1 tsp ginger pulp
5ml/1 tsp garlic pulp
5ml/1 tsp ground coriander
5ml/1 tsp chilli powder
5ml/1 tsp salt
175ml/6fl oz/¾ cup water
15ml/1 tbsp lemon juice
2.5ml/½ tsp soft light brown sugar
15ml/1 tbsp chopped fresh coriander (cilantro)
1 tomato, diced
fresh chapati and a daal dish, to serve

1 Prepare the okra by washing it, then top and tail it and slice it into roughly 1cm/½in-pieces.

2 Heat the oil in a medium wok or frying pan over a medium heat. Add the tomato paste, followed by the ginger, garlic, ground coriander, chilli powder and salt. Stir to combine.

3 Add the sliced okra, lower the heat and stir-fry for 8–10 minutes.

4 Add the water, lower the heat further, and cover and cook for about 2 minutes until the okra is tender.

5 Stir in the lemon juice, brown sugar, fresh coriander and the diced tomato. Serve warm with chapati and a daal dish.

TARKA DAAL

CLASSIC TARKA DAAL

Daal is served daily in the majority of households as an accompaniment to most meals, and this simple yet versatile one is a favourite all over Pakistan. The daal element comprises two types of lentil, which are cooked with spices and then processed until smooth. A tarka, made by frying onions and spices in ghee, is then poured over the lentils, lending flavour as well as texture to the finished dish.

SERVES 4

115g/4oz/½ cup chana daal
225g/8oz/1 cup masoor daal
750ml/1¼ pints/3 cups water
5ml/1 tsp ginger pulp
5ml/1 tsp garlic pulp
7.5ml/1½ tsp chilli powder
1.5ml/¼ tsp ground turmeric
7.5ml/1½ tsp salt
5ml/1 tsp ground coriander
5ml/1 tsp garam masala
30ml/2 tbsp lemon juice
a few sprigs of fresh coriander (cilantro), to garnish

FOR THE TARKA

30ml/2 tbsp vegetable ghee
1 onion, peeled and diced
2.5ml/½ tsp white cumin seeds
15ml/1 tbsp chopped fresh coriander (cilantro)

1 Put both types of daal in a large bowl of cold water, then drain, rinse again in more water, and drain again.

2 Put the daals into a large pan, then add the water, ginger, garlic, chilli powder and ground turmeric. Cook over a medium-low heat for about 25 minutes, until both the daals are soft. Insert a spoon in the pan to prevent the mixture from boiling over.

3 Remove from the heat and use a deep ladle to spoon half of the daal into a food processor or blender. Process until the lentils are smooth and thick.

4 Pour the processed lentils back into the pan and mix with the chunkier cooked lentils. Add the salt, ground coriander, garam masala and lemon juice. Mix well and transfer to a serving dish.

5 To make the tarka, heat the vegetable ghee in a frying pan over a medium heat. Add the onion and cumin seeds and fry for 10–15 minutes, until the onion is soft and golden brown. Pour the tarka over the daal and serve garnished with fresh coriander.

MAASH KI DAAL

SPICED URID TARKA DAAL

Served almost like a gravy, a moist accompaniment to many main meals, daals are nearly infinite in their variety and Pakistani home cooks will often have a closely guarded family recipe up their sleeves. This particular one is almost always served with freshly made chapatis, either alongside other dishes or simply on its own for a nutritious vegetarian meal.

SERVES 4

225g/8oz/1 cup urid daal
750ml/1¼ pints/3 cups water
5ml/1 tsp ginger pulp
5ml/1 tsp garlic pulp
5ml/1 tsp salt
5ml/1 tsp coarsely ground black pepper
chapatis, to serve

FOR THE TARKA

30ml/2 tbsp vegetable ghee
30ml/2 tbsp butter
½ onion, finely sliced

FOR THE GARNISH

2.5cm/1½in piece of fresh root ginger, peeled and thinly sliced
2 fresh green chillies
4–6 fresh mint leaves
2.5ml/½ tsp chaat masala

1 Put the urid daal in a large bowl of cold water, then drain, rinse again in more water, and drain again.

2 Put the daal into a medium pan, then add the water and cook over a medium heat for 15–20 minutes. Insert a spoon in the pan to prevent the mixture from boiling over.

3 Add the ginger, garlic, salt and pepper, and continue to cook with the pan part-covered with a lid, until the mixture is soft but not totally dry, pouring in a little more water if necessary so you get a slightly runny and sticky texture. Remove from the heat and transfer to a serving dish.

4 For the tarka, heat the ghee and butter in a frying pan over a medium-high heat and fry the onions for 10–15 minutes, until golden brown and almost crispy.

5 Pour the tarka over the top of the daal, then garnish with the ginger, fresh chillies and mint leaves. Finally sprinkle over the chaat masala and serve with some chapatis.

DAAL MAKHANI
CREAMY BLACK LENTIL DAAL

This is a typical Punjabi provincial recipe that uses whole black lentils (black gram), kidney beans and butter for a rich flavour. Pouring over a little cream before serving the dish gives it a particularly appetizing look and accentuates the luscious texture.

SERVES 4

- 350/12oz/1½ cups whole black gram
- 115g/4oz/½ cup butter
- 60ml/4 tbsp vegetable oil
- 2 medium onions, peeled and finely diced
- 10ml/2 tsp garlic pulp
- 10ml/2 tsp ginger pulp
- 12.5ml/2½ tsp chilli powder
- 2.5ml/½ tsp ground turmeric
- 10ml/2 tsp ground coriander
- 7.5–10ml/1½–2 tsp salt
- 10ml/2 tsp garam masala, plus a pinch to garnish
- 2 medium fresh tomatoes, sliced
- 200g/7oz canned red kidney beans, drained
- 1 litre/1¾ pints/4 cups water

FOR THE GARNISH

- 45–60ml/3–4 tbsp single (light) cream
- 2 each fresh green and red chillies, chopped
- 15ml/1 tbsp chopped fresh coriander (cilantro)
- 2.5cm/1in-piece of fresh root ginger, sliced
- 15ml/1 tbsp lemon juice
- plain boiled rice or roti, to serve

1 Wash the whole black gram in a strainer, then tip into a bowl and cover with cold water. Leave to soak overnight, as this will help to reduce the cooking time.

2 Heat the butter with the oil in a large pan, then add the onions and fry for 10–15 minutes, until soft and golden brown.

3 Add the garlic, ginger, chilli powder, ground turmeric and coriander, salt, 10ml/2 tsp garam masala and the sliced tomatoes and stir to combine.

4 Drain the black gram, then add them to the pan with the drained canned kidney beans. Stir to combine and cook for 5–7 minutes.

5 Pour in the water and cook for 20–25 minutes over a medium heat, until more than half of the water is absorbed and the daal has a thickish consistency.

6 Taste and adjust the seasoning as necessary and transfer to a serving dish.

7 Garnish with the cream, fresh chillies, fresh coriander and sliced fresh ginger and sprinkle with a pinch of garam masala. Finally, sprinkle over the lemon juice and serve with plain boiled rice or roti.

RICE, BREADS & ACCOMPANIMENTS

RECIPES

SUBZEE KA PULAO
VEGETABLE RICE

CHANA PULAO
CHICKPEA RICE

MASALA JHINGA PULAO
SPICY PRAWN RICE

MURGH TIKKA BIRYANI
CHICKEN TIKKA BIRYANI

SINDHI BIRYANI MURGH
SINDHI CHICKEN BIRYANI

MUTTON BIRYANI
MUTTON BIRYANI

MATAR PULAO RICE
GREEN PEA PULAO RICE

PUNJABI CHAAM KA PULAO
PUNJABI-STYLE CHOPS PULAO

ALOO PARATHA
SPICED POTATO-FILLED FLAKY BREAD

NAAN
TANDOORI LEAVENED BREAD

KHAJOOR AUR IMLI KI CHUTNEY
DATE AND TAMARIND CHUTNEY

PODINAY AUR KAIRI KI CHUTNEY
MINT AND RAW MANGO CHUTNEY

SUBZEE KA PULAO
VEGETABLE RICE

Rice studded with finely chopped fresh vegetables and flavoured with classic mild spices is a ubiquitous sight at Pakistani tables, where it makes the ideal partner to practically any curry. For speed and convenience this version uses mixed frozen vegetables, but you can just finely dice whatever you have to hand; courgettes (zucchini) or small cauliflower florets would work perfectly well, just make sure you don't overcook them.

1 Wash the rice in a strainer until the water runs clear, then tip it into a bowl and add enough cold water to cover. Leave to soak for about 30 minutes.

2 Heat the ghee in a pan over a medium-high heat, then add the onion and fry for about 5 minutes, until it is starting to soften.

3 Add the garlic and ginger pulp, followed by the curry leaves, onion seeds and mustard seeds. Add the vegetables and the yogurt and stir-fry for 5–7 minutes.

4 Stir in the pepper, fresh coriander, salt and rice and stir for about 2 minutes before adding the water.

5 Mix well, then cover the pan with a lid. Lower the heat to medium and cook the rice for 15–20 minutes, checking it at least once so that the rice does not catch on the bottom of the pan.

6 Remove from the heat and leave to stand for 10 minutes before serving.

SERVES 4

300g/11oz/1½ cups basmati rice
45ml/3 tbsp vegetable ghee
1 small onion, peeled and sliced
2.5ml/½ tsp garlic pulp
2.5ml/½ tsp ginger pulp
4–6 curry leaves
2.5ml/½ tsp onion seeds
2.5ml/½ tsp mustard seeds
115g/4oz frozen mixed vegetables (such as carrots, peas, corn and beans), thawed, or the equivalent quantity of prepared fresh vegetables
30ml/2 tbsp natural (plain) yogurt
½ each red and green (bell) pepper, seeded and finely diced
15ml/1 tbsp chopped fresh coriander (cilantro)
5ml/1 tsp salt
750ml/1¼ pints/3 cups water

CHANA PULAO
CHICKPEA RICE

Chana Pulao is a classic Punjabi dish that is a popular feature at the festival of Lohri, which takes place on the day of the winter solstice. It is very easy to prepare and deserves to be made more frequently, just make sure you always use good-quality basmati rice as it really makes a difference to the end result. This rice dish is a good accompaniment to most curries.

SERVES 4

300g/11oz/1½ cups basmati rice
30ml/2 tbsp vegetable ghee
2 bay leaves
6 black peppercorns
2–3 black cardamoms
5ml/1 tsp ginger pulp
5ml/1 tsp garlic pulp
7.5ml/1½ tsp salt
750ml/1 pints/3 cups water
400g/14oz canned chickpeas, drained

1 Wash the rice in a strainer until the water runs clear, then set aside.

2 Heat the ghee in a pan over a medium heat, then add the bay leaf, peppercorns, cardamoms, ginger, garlic, salt and drained rice.

3 Stir around gently using a slotted steel spoon for about 1 minute.

4 Reduce the heat to low, then add water and chickpeas. Cover the pan with a lid and cook for 10–12 minutes, until the water has been absorbed and the rice is cooked.

5 Turn off the heat and leave the rice to stand for 10–15 minutes before fluffing up the rice with a slotted spoon and serving.

MASALA JHINGA PULAO

SPICY PRAWN RICE

Aromatic and colourful, this tasty rice dish can be eaten on its own or as part of a larger spread. Chinese food is very popular in Pakistan, so this sort of stir-fried dish is commonly enjoyed all over the country and probably has its origins in the Chinese tradition, albeit with a Pakistani twist. If you prefer you can use fresh vegetables rather than frozen.

SERVES 4–6

200g/7oz/1 cup basmati rice
45ml/3 tbsp vegetable oil
15ml/1 tbsp sesame oil
3 spring onions (scallions), chopped
5ml/1 tsp ginger pulp
5ml/1 tsp garlic pulp
5ml/1 tsp crushed dried red chillies
2.5ml/½ tsp onion seeds
115g/4oz frozen mixed vegetables (such as carrots, peas, corn and beans), thawed, or the equivalent quantity of prepared fresh vegetables
1 each red and green (bell) pepper, seeded and diced
5ml/1 tsp salt
8–12 raw king prawns (jumbo shrimp), shelled and deveined if necessary
475ml/16fl oz/2 cups water
raita, to serve (optional)

1 Wash the rice thoroughly in a strainer until the water runs clear, then set aside.

2 Heat the vegetable and sesame oils in a pan over a medium-high heat. Add the spring onions, ginger, garlic, crushed dried red chillies, onion seeds, mixed vegetables, diced peppers and salt.

3 Blend everything together, then add the drained rice, prawns and water. Gently stir to combine everything well.

4 Reduce the heat to medium, cover the pan and cook for 10 minutes, until the water is absorbed and the rice and prawns are cooked.

5 Remove the pan from the heat and leave the rice to stand for 10 minutes. Fluff up the rice with a slotted spoon or fork and serve with raita, if you like.

MURGH TIKKA BIRYANI
CHICKEN TIKKA BIRYANI

This eye-catching biryani makes a great dinner-party piece. Tikka is eaten widely all over Pakistan and is a national favourite. Many recipes use chicken on the bone, but this one uses chicken breast fillets for ease of eating.

SERVES 4

1 medium onion, peeled and rough chopped
300g/11oz/1½ cups basmati rice
6–8 whole black peppercorns
1cm/½in piece of cinnamon stick
3 whole green cardamoms
7.5ml/1½ tsp black cumin seeds
60ml/4 tbsp whole natural (plain) yogurt
7.5ml/1½ tsp ginger pulp
7.5ml/1½ tsp garlic pulp
10ml/2 tsp chilli powder
7.5ml/1½ tsp ground cumin
7.5ml/1½ tsp ground coriander
2.5ml/½ tsp ground turmeric
7.5ml/1½ tsp garam masala
5ml/1 tsp salt, or to taste
30ml/2 tbsp lemon juice
2 large skinless chicken breast fillets, cut into cubes
60ml/4 tbsp vegetable ghee
raita, to serve

TO GARNISH

a pinch of saffron
120ml/4fl oz/½ cup hot milk
90ml/6 tbsp vegetable ghee
30ml/2 tbsp lemon juice
15ml/1 tbsp chopped fresh coriander (cilantro)
1 tomato, sliced

1 Put the onion in a food processor and process until it forms a pulp.

2 Wash the rice in a strainer until the water runs clear, then tip it into a bowl and add enough cold water to cover, along with the peppercorns, cinnamon stick, cardamoms and black cumin seeds. Leave to soak for about 30 minutes.

3 In a separate bowl, mix together the yogurt, ginger, garlic, chilli powder, ground cumin, coriander and turmeric, garam masala, salt, lemon juice and chicken. Stir to combine and set aside for 30 minutes to marinate.

4 Heat the ghee in a large wok or heavy frying pan, add the onion pulp and fry for about 10 minutes, until golden brown, stirring occasionally.

5 Add the marinated chicken and the marinade to the wok or pan and cook, stirring, for about 10 minutes, until the mixture is semi-dry and the chicken is cooked through. Set aside.

6 Meanwhile, for the garnish, put the saffron in a small bowl with the hot milk and leave it to steep. Melt the ghee and leave it to cool slightly.

7 Drain the rice and put it in a pan along with the spices with which it was soaked. Pour in enough cold water to cover, bring to a simmer and cook the rice over a medium heat for 3–5 minutes, until it is par-cooked. Check the rice by rubbing the grains between your thumb and index finger; it should feel slightly undercooked. Drain the rice through a strainer.

8 Transfer half of the rice back into the pan and spread it out in an even layer. Pour the chicken mixture over the top of the rice, spreading it out to form an even layer, then top this with the remaining rice to form a top layer.

9 Garnish the rice with the fresh coriander and sliced tomato. Stir the melted ghee into the saffron-infused milk, and pour this and the lemon juice over the rice.

10 Cover the pan with a clean, damp dish towel and then a tight-fitting lid, and steam-cook over a medium heat for 15–20 minutes, until steam begins to escape from the lid.

11 Leave the biryani to stand for about 15 minutes before serving it with raita.

SINDHI BIRYANI MURGH
SINDHI CHICKEN BIRYANI

This biryani has become very popular in recent years, especially in Karachi, which is part of the Sindh province. It is quite spicy compared to other biryanis and can be made using lamb, fish or, as here, chicken on the bone, which is the traditional way. If you prefer you can use cubed chicken breast fillets.

1 Wash the rice in a strainer until the water runs clear, then tip it into a bowl and add enough cold water to cover. Leave to soak for about 30 minutes.

2 Put the yogurt in a bowl and stir in the chilli powder, ginger, garlic, ground coriander, garam masala, ground cardamom, salt and prunes. Stir in the chicken, cover and set aside to marinate for about 30 minutes.

3 Heat the ghee in a medium pan over a medium heat, add the onions, cloves, peppercorns, cinnamon stick and bay leaf and fry for about 10 minutes, until the onion is golden brown.

4 Remove about 30ml/2 tbsp of the ghee and onion mixture and set it aside. Add the chicken with its marinade to the remaining onions in the pan and stir well to combine.

5 Add enough water to cover the chicken, along with the potatoes, carrots and tomatoes. Cover the pan and cook for 15–20 minutes, stirring occasionally. Remove from the heat and set aside.

6 Meanwhile, for the garnish, put the saffron in a small bowl with the hot milk and leave it to steep. Heat the oil in a frying pan, add the sliced onion and fry for about 10 minutes, until it is golden brown.

7 Drain the rice and put it in a pan along with the salt. Pour in enough cold water to cover, bring to a simmer and cook over a medium heat for 3–5 minutes, until the rice is par-cooked. Check the rice by rubbing the grains between your thumb and index finger; it should feel slightly undercooked. Drain the rice through a strainer.

8 Transfer half of the rice back into the pan and spread it out in an even layer. Pour the chicken mixture over the top of the rice, spreading it out to form an even layer, then top this with the remaining rice to form a top layer.

9 To garnish, spread out the fried onion on top of the rice layer along with the ghee, fresh chillies, fresh coriander, saffron-infused milk and lemon juice.

10 Cover the pan with a clean, damp dish towel and then a tight-fitting lid and steam-cook over a medium heat for 15–20 minutes, until steam begins to escape from the lid.

11 Leave the biryani to stand for about 15 minutes before serving it with raita.

SERVES 4

400g/14oz/2 cups basmati rice
60ml/4 tbsp whole natural (plain) yogurt
7.5ml/1½ tsp chilli powder
7.5ml/1½ tsp ginger pulp
7.5ml/1½ tsp garlic pulp
7.5ml/1½ tsp ground coriander
10ml/2 tsp garam masala
2.5ml/½ tsp ground cardamom
5ml/1 tsp salt
6 canned prunes, drained
1 baby chicken, skinned and cut into 8–10 pieces on the bone (see page 62)
150g/5oz/10 tbsp vegetable ghee
3 medium onions, peeled and sliced
4 cloves
6–8 black peppercorns
4cm/1½in piece of cinnamon stick
1 bay leaf
about 120ml/4fl oz/½ cup water, plus extra for soaking and cooking the rice
2 medium potatoes, peeled and cut into large wedges
2 carrots, peeled and sliced
2 tomatoes, quartered
10ml/2 tsp salt
raita, to serve

TO GARNISH
a large pinch of saffron
120ml/4fl oz/½ cup hot milk
15ml/1 tbsp vegetable oil
½ onion, peeled and sliced
30ml/2 tbsp vegetable ghee
3 each fresh green and red chillies, split lengthwise and seeded
15ml/1 tbsp chopped fresh coriander (cilantro)
30–45ml/2–3 tbsp lemon juice

MUTTON BIRYANI
MUTTON BIRYANI

Biryanis are a must at festive occasions, especially weddings, although they are enjoyed at other times too. They can be made using chicken, lamb, seafood or vegetables. For this version, mutton on the bone is cut into pieces and marinated overnight for maximum flavour.

1 In a large bowl, thoroughly combine the mutton, yogurt, ginger, garlic, ground coriander, garam masala, chilli powder, ground turmeric, almonds, cardamom and cloves, whole green cardamoms and salt. Cover and leave to marinate in the refrigerator for at least 4 hours and ideally overnight.

2 For the garnish, put the milk and saffron in bowl and set aside to steep.

3 Heat the ghee in a large pan over a medium heat. Add the onions and cook for 10–15 minutes, until soft and golden brown. Remove half the onions and ghee from the pan, place them in a bowl and set aside for the garnish.

4 Return the pan containing the remaining ghee and onions to the heat and add the meat and its marinade. Stir-fry for about 10 minutes, until the meat is sealed.

5 Add the water and cook over a medium heat for about 45 minutes, stirring occasionally and checking to see if the meat is cooked and tender. Add a further 100ml/3½fl oz/ scant ½ cup water if necessary.

6 Once the meat is cooked, stir-fry the mixture for a further 5 minutes, until it is semi-dry. Set aside.

7 Meanwhile, wash the rice in a strainer until the water runs clear, then tip it into a pan with the cinnamon, peppercorns, cloves and black cumin seeds. Pour in enough cold water to cover, bring to a simmer and cook over a medium heat for 3–5 minutes, until the rice is par-cooked. Check the rice by rubbing the grains between your thumb and index finger; it should feel slightly undercooked. Drain through a strainer.

8 Transfer half of the rice back into the pan and spread it out in an even layer. Pour the mutton mixture over the top of the rice, spreading it out to form an even layer, then top this with the remaining rice to form a top layer.

9 To garnish, sprinkle the top of the rice with the saffron-infused milk, orange food colouring (if using), lemon juice, fresh green chillies, fresh coriander and the reserved fried onions. Finally, sprinkle over the kewra water.

10 Cover the pan with a clean, damp dish towel and then a tight-fitting lid and steam-cook over a medium heat for 15–20 minutes, until steam begins to escape from the lid.

11 Leave the biryani to stand for about 15 minutes before gently mixing it using a slotted spoon. Serve with raita.

SERVES 4

- 1kg/2¼lb lean mutton on the bone, cut into 5cm/2in cubes
- 120ml/4fl oz/½ cup whole natural (plain) yogurt
- 10ml/2 tsp ginger pulp
- 10ml/2 tsp garlic pulp
- 10ml/2 tsp ground coriander
- 10ml/2 tsp garam masala
- 10ml/2 tsp chilli powder
- 2.5ml/½ tsp ground turmeric
- 30ml/2 tbsp ground almonds
- 5ml/1 tsp ground cardamom
- 1.5ml/¼ tsp ground cloves
- 4 whole green cardamoms
- 10ml/2 tsp salt
- 115g/4oz/½ cup vegetable ghee
- 3 medium onions, peeled and sliced
- about 600ml/1 pint/2½ cups water, plus extra for cooking the rice
- 500g/1¼lb/2½ cups basmati rice
- 2.5cm/1in piece of cinnamon stick
- 8–10 black peppercorns
- 4 cloves
- 5ml/1 tsp black cumin seeds
- raita, to serve

TO GARNISH

- 150ml/¼ pint/⅔ cup hot milk
- 2.5ml/½ tsp saffron strands
- 1.5ml/¼ tsp orange food colouring (optional)
- 120–150ml/4fl oz–¼ pint/ ½–⅔ cup lemon juice
- 4 fresh green chillies, finely chopped
- 45ml/3 tbsp chopped fresh coriander (cilantro)
- a few drops of kewra water

MATAR PULAO RICE
GREEN PEA PULAO RICE

There are several ways of making pulao rice, but this one is very adaptable and produces an aromatic result. It's particularly enjoyable when served with a garnish of fried dried onions, and makes a wonderful accompaniment to all manner of dishes.

SERVES 4

200g/7oz/1 cup basmati rice
30ml/2 tbsp vegetable ghee
15ml/1 tbsp vegetable oil
4 green cardamoms
3–4 whole cloves
5ml/1 tsp ginger pulp
5ml/1 tsp garlic pulp
1 onion, peeled and sliced
5ml/1 tsp salt or to taste
50g/2oz/½ cup frozen peas
475ml/16fl oz/2 cups water

TO GARNISH

30–45ml/2–3 tbsp vegetable oil
15ml/1 tbsp dried onions
15ml/1 tbsp chopped fresh coriander (cilantro)
1 tomato, sliced

1 Wash the rice in a strainer until the water runs clear, then set aside.

2 Heat the ghee and oil in a pan over a medium heat, then add the cardamoms, cloves, ginger, garlic, onion and salt and fry for 10–15 minutes, until the onion is soft and golden brown.

3 Add the washed rice and peas and gently stir to combine. Stir in the water and reduce the heat to medium-low.

4 Cover the pan and cook the rice for 10–12 minutes, until the water is fully absorbed and the rice is cooked. Remove the pan from the heat and leave it to stand for about 10 minutes.

5 Meanwhile, prepare the garnish. Heat the oil in a frying pan over a medium heat, then add the dried onions and fry them for just a few seconds, until crispy. Watch them as they cook as they burn very quickly.

6 Fluff up the rice with a fork or slotted spoon, then serve garnished with the fried onions, fresh coriander and tomato slices.

PUNJABI CHAAM KA PULAO

PUNJABI-STYLE CHOPS PULAO

This is a very typically Lahori pulao that is best enjoyed simply with a raita so the rich flavour of the rice and meat can shine through. Although the flavours may be complex, the dish itself is relatively easier to make than a standard biryani, as no layering is involved.

SERVES 4

90ml/6 tbsp vegetable ghee
2 medium onions, peeled and sliced
2 bay leaves
8–10 black peppercorns
2.5cm/1in piece of cinnamon stick
6 green cardamoms
5ml/1 tsp crushed coriander seeds
2.5ml/½ tsp white cumin seeds
60ml/4 tbsp whole natural (plain) yogurt
7.5ml/1½ tsp ginger pulp
7.5ml/1½ tsp garlic pulp
5ml/1 tsp chilli powder
5ml/1 tsp crushed dried red chillies
5ml/1 tsp ground coriander
5ml/1 tsp garam masala
5ml/1 tsp ground cardamom
7.5ml/1½ tsp salt
500g/1¼lb spring lamb chops, trimmed of fat
400g/14oz/2 cups basmati rice, rinsed thoroughly and drained
750ml/1¼ pints/3 cups water
15ml/1 tbsp chopped fresh coriander (cilantro)
2–3 fresh green chillies
1 lemon, cut into thin wedges
raita, to serve

1 Heat the vegetable ghee in a large pan over a medium heat. Add the onions, bay leaves, peppercorns, cinnamon, cardamoms and the coriander and cumin seeds and fry for 10–15 minutes, until the onion is soft and golden brown.

2 Meanwhile, put the yogurt in a large bowl and stir in the ginger, garlic, chilli powder, crushed dried red chillies, ground coriander, garam masala, ground cardamom and salt. Add the chops and stir to coat them thoroughly.

3 Add the chops and the yogurt mixture to the pan containing the onions and stir-fry for 2 minutes. Add 250ml/8fl oz/1 cup of the water, reduce the heat to low, then cover and cook 25–30 minutes or until the water has evaporated, stirring occasionally using semi-circular movements.

4 Add the rice and stir using a slotted spoon, then add the remaining water, half of the fresh coriander, half of the fresh green chillies and the lemon wedges. Re-cover the pan and cook for a further 8–10 minutes, until the water has been fully absorbed and the rice is cooked through.

5 Remove from the heat and leave to stand for 10–15 minutes before garnishing with the remaining fresh coriander and fresh green chillies and serving with raita.

ALOO PARATHA
SPICED POTATO-FILLED FLAKY BREAD

The type of bread known as paratha is traditionally a rich, unleavened bread that can be plain or stuffed. This version, aloo paratha, is filled with spiced potatoes, and heart-healthy olive oil or just some vegetable oil is used instead of the more traditional ghee or butter.

MAKES 8

- 450g/1lb/4 cups wholemeal (whole-wheat) bread flour, plus extra for dusting
- 2.5ml/½ tsp salt, or to taste
- 30ml/2 tbsp vegetable oil or light olive oil, plus extra for shallow-frying
- 290ml/9fl oz/scant 1⅓ cups warm water

FOR THE FILLING

- 15ml/1 tbsp vegetable oil or light olive oil
- 2.5ml/½ tsp black or brown mustard seeds
- 2 shallots, finely chopped
- 10ml/2 tsp ginger pulp
- 1 fresh green chilli, finely chopped (deseeded if preferred)
- 30ml/2 tbsp finely chopped fresh coriander (cilantro)
- 2.5ml/½ tsp salt, or to taste
- 225g/8oz potatoes, boiled in their skins then peeled and mashed

1 Put the flour and salt in a bowl and work in the 30ml/2 tbsp oil with your fingertips. Gradually add the water and mix until a soft dough is formed.

2 Transfer the dough to a lightly floured surface and knead for 3–4 minutes or until all traces of stickiness disappear. Alternatively, put all the ingredients into a food processor with a dough hook and run the machine for about 5 minutes, until the dough feels soft and there is no stickiness.

3 Cover the dough with a damp dish towel and set aside for 30 minutes.

4 Meanwhile, prepare the filling. Heat the oil over a medium heat and add the mustard seeds. As soon as they start popping, add the shallot, ginger and fresh green chilli.

5 Stir-fry for 2–3 minutes, then stir in the fresh coriander and salt and remove from the heat. Transfer to a large bowl. Add the mashed potato to this mixture and stir well.

6 Divide the dough into 2 equal parts and make 4 portions out of each. Shape each portion into a ball and flatten it into a smooth cake.

7 Form each dough cake into a saucer shape by gently stretching, and moisten the edges with cold water. Place a portion of the filling in each, bring up the sides of the dough and seal the edges by pressing them together. Press the ball to form a flat cake.

8 Preheat a cast-iron griddle or other heavy frying pan over a medium heat. Dust each of the flat cakes with flour and, with gentle pressure, roll out to a 15cm/6in disc.

9 Place one disc on the hot griddle and cook for 1 minute, then turn it over and cook the other side for 1 minute. Spread 5ml/1 tsp oil on the cooked side, turn it over and spread oil on the other side. Flip it over again and cook the side that was oiled first for 2–3 minutes, until brown patches appear.

10 Turn over the disc and cook the other side for a further 2–3 minutes, until brown patches appear. Place the paratha on a piece of foil lined with kitchen paper. Cover while you cook the remaining parathas in the same way.

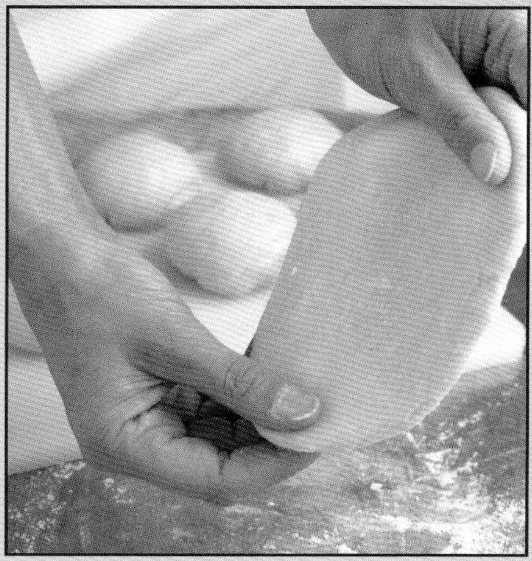

NAAN
TANDOORI LEAVENED BREAD

Meaning simply 'bread' in Urdu, naan are more often than not bought from street vendors or bakeries in Pakistan rather than being made at home, since the real deal requires a tandoor oven. That said, a close approximation can be created in a domestic setting, and these ones certainly taste better than mass-produced naan bought from a supermarket. Although available in many guises, this plain version, saada naan, is the most versatile and is typically served with dishes such as nehari.

SERVES 4

500g/1¼lb/4½ cups self-raising (self-rising) flour, plus extra for dusting
5ml/1 tsp baking powder
5ml/1 tsp salt
10ml/2 tsp sugar
50g/2oz/4 tbsp softened butter, plus extra for brushing
250ml/8fl oz/1 cup warm milk
oil, for greasing
melted butter, to glaze

1 Sift the flour into a large mixing bowl and stir in the baking powder, salt and sugar. Rub in the butter, then add the milk and mix until a dough is formed.

2 Transfer the dough to a lightly floured pastry board and knead for 10 minutes, until it is soft and pliable. Shape the dough into a ball, cover with a damp cloth and leave it to rest for 30 minutes.

3 Preheat the grill or broiler to high and heat it for 8–10 minutes, then line a grill pan with a piece of foil and brush it with a little oil.

4 Divide the dough into 8 equal-sized portions, then form each of these into a cake. Roll each cake into a circle 13cm/5in in diameter, then gently pull the lower end to form it into the traditional teardrop shape. Roll again, maintaining the teardrop shape, to form a 23cm/9in naan.

5 Place a naan in the prepared grill pan and cook it 13cm/5in below the heat source for about 1½ minutes, until it puffs up. Keep an eye on it as it can burn easily when it puffs up if it gets too close to the heat element in the grill.

6 Turn it over and grill for a further minute or until brown patches appear.

7 Place the cooked naan on a clean dish towel and brush the surface with a little melted butter. Wrap it in the towel to keep it hot and soft while you cook the other naans in the same way.

8 Serve warm with any meat, poultry or vegetable curry dish.

VARIATIONS Before cooking the naan, brush with a little beaten egg and sprinkle on flavourings such as sesame seeds, cumin seeds, nigella seeds, poppy seeds, chopped garlic, chopped fresh green chillies or fresh coriander (cilantro).

KHAJOOR AUR IMLI KI CHUTNEY
DATE AND TAMARIND CHUTNEY

This chutney has a delicious and delightful sweet-and-sour flavour from the sweet dates and lemony tamarind. It can be served as a tasty dip for snacks or appetizers or as an accompaniment to any meal.

1 Roughly chop the dates, then put them in a strainer with the sultanas. Rinse the dried fruits under running water.

2 Transfer to a heavy pan and add the water. Bring to the boil and simmer for 5–7 minutes, until the fruits are softened and turning into a paste.

3 Remove the pan from the heat and add the tamarind paste, sugar, chilli powder, ground coriander, cumin and ginger, salt and vinegar.

4 Stir to combine, then return the pan to the heat and simmer for 1–2 minutes over a medium heat.

5 Transfer the mixture to a food processor and process it for about 30 seconds, adding a drop of water if necessary. The consistency should resemble thick tomato ketchup.

6 Place the chutney in a serving bowl, or transfer it to a sterilized jar and keep it in the refrigerator for up to 2 weeks.

SERVES 8–12

200g/8oz/2⅔ cups dates, pitted
30ml/2 tbsp sultanas (golden raisins)
300ml/½ pint/1¼ cups hot water
15ml/1 tbsp red tamarind paste
30ml/2 tbsp soft light brown sugar
5ml/1 tsp chilli powder
10ml/2 tsp ground coriander
5ml/1 tsp ground cumin
5ml/1 tsp ground ginger
5ml/1 tsp salt
45ml/3 tbsp brown malt vinegar

SERVES 4

1 large mango
90–120ml/6–8 tbsp fresh mint leaves
60ml/4 tbsp fresh coriander (cilantro)
2–3 fresh green chillies
2 garlic cloves
2.5ml/½ tsp salt
5ml/1 tsp soft light brown sugar
15ml/1 tbsp lemon juice
30ml/2 tbsp water

PODINAY AUR KAIRI KI CHUTNEY

MINT AND RAW MANGO CHUTNEY

This tangy, versatile and delicious chutney is eaten either as a part of a main meal or as a tasty accompaniment to any snack. Furthermore, it makes a mouthwatering sandwich spread.

1 Cut away the mango flesh from the stone or pit, then peel the skin with a peeler or sharp knife and roughly chop the flesh.

2 Roughly chop the fresh mint and coriander and put them, together with the mango, into a food processor. Add the fresh green chillies, garlic cloves, salt, sugar, lemon juice and water. Process for about 2 minutes or until the paste is smooth in texture. Taste and adjust the seasoning as necessary. Add more sugar if the chutney seems sour.

3 Place the chutney in a serving bowl, or transfer it to a sterilized jar and keep it in the refrigerator for up to 2 weeks.

DESSERTS & DRINKS

RECIPES

ZARDA
SWEET SAFFRON RICE

AAM KI KEER
MANGO RICE PUDDING

SOOJI KA HALVA
SEMOLINA DESSERT

SHEER KORMA
VERMICELLI DESSERT

GAJAR KA HALVA
CARROT DESSERT

SHAHI TUKRAY
BREAD PUDDING – PAKISTANI-STYLE

BADAM SHERBET
ALMOND SHERBET

GULAAB KAY SHEERAY KI LASSI
ROSE SYRUP LASSI

ZAFRANI DOODH PATTI
SPICED SAFFRON TEA

ZARDA
SWEET SAFFRON RICE

Zarda is a traditional dessert that is quick and easy to make and looks very impressive, especially when it is decorated with pistachio nuts and warq for a special occasion, such as a wedding. The word 'zard' means 'yellow' in Urdu, in reference to the golden colour imparted by the saffron, although in many cases yellow food dye is also used. A variation on this bright rice theme is mutanjan, a similar recipe in which small batches of rice are dyed different colours and then mixed with vibrant-hued candied fruits and some nuts to give a technicoloured effect.

SERVES 4

200g/7oz/1 cup basmati rice
200g/7oz/1 cup sugar
a pinch of saffron strands
300ml/½ pint/1¼ cups water, plus extra for soaking and cooking the rice
30ml/2 tbsp pure ghee
3 whole cloves
3 whole green cardamoms
25g/1oz/⅕ cup sultanas (golden raisins)
cream, to serve (optional)

TO GARNISH

a few unsalted pistachio nut kernels
warq (silver leaf)

1 Wash the rice under cold running water, drain, then wash it again. Put it into a pan and pour in enough cold water to cover. Bring to a simmer and cook over a medium heat for 3–5 minutes, until the rice is par-cooked. Check the rice by rubbing the grains between your thumb and index finger; it should feel slightly undercooked. Drain the rice through a strainer.

2 Put the sugar, saffron and water in a separate pan and place over a medium heat until the sugar dissolves. Do not stir. Increase the heat once the sugar has dissolved and boil until the syrup thickens but does not brown. Set aside.

3 Heat the ghee in another pan over a medium heat, then add the cloves and cardamoms and cook for 1–2 minutes. Remove from the heat.

4 Return the rice to a low heat, add the sultanas and pour over the sugar syrup. Stir to combine, then pour over the ghee and spices and simmer over a low heat for 10–15 minutes, stirring frequently. Check to see whether the rice is cooked; if not, add a little water, cover and simmer until it is soft.

5 Garnish with pistachio nuts and warq, and serve warm, with cream if desired.

AAM KI KEER
MANGO RICE PUDDING

Mangoes are very seasonal, only being available in the summer before the monsoon season begins in Pakistan. During this time there is almost a nationwide mango festival, with the fruit being used to make desserts, soufflés, ice creams and milkshakes, or eaten on their own.

1 Wash the basmati rice in a strainer until the water runs clear, then place it in a grinder and process briefly until the rice is coarse but not powdered.

2 Put the ground rice in a large pan and add 600ml/1 pint/2½ cups of the milk along with the cardamoms. Bring to the boil over a low heat then simmer gently for about 10–15 minutes, stirring occasionally, until the milk has been absorbed.

3 Remove from the heat, scoop out the cardamoms and mash the cooked rice. Return to the heat, add the remaining milk and mix in really well. Stir in the sugar and the ground almonds and cook over a medium heat, stirring occasionally for about 15 minutes. When the rice pudding reaches the consistency of a thick soup, remove it from the heat, pour it into a serving dish and set aside to cool.

4 Meanwhile, cut away the mango flesh from the stones (pits), peel off the skin and then dice the flesh finely, almost to a pulp.

5 Put the whole almonds in a small heatproof bowl and pour over enough boiling water to cover. Leave to soak for 1–2 minutes, until the skins look baggy, then drain the hot water and replace it with cold water. Leave for 1 minute, then drain the almonds and pop them out of their skins, which should now come away easily. Slither the almonds into fine pieces.

6 Stir the chopped mango and the cream into the pudding, then garnish with the almonds. For a special occasion, you could decorate the top with rose petals.

SERVES 4

- 75g/3oz/⅜ cup basmati rice
- 1.2 litres/2 pints/5 cups full-fat (whole) milk
- 4 whole green cardamoms
- 90g/3½oz/½ cup sugar
- 15ml/1 tbsp ground almonds
- 2 ripe Pakistani mangoes, such as Anwar Ratul, Chaunsa or any good variety
- 15–20 whole almonds
- 30–45ml/2–3 tbsp double (heavy) cream
- red rose petals, to garnish (optional)

SERVES 4

90ml/6 tbsp pure ghee
3 whole cloves
3 whole green cardamoms
75g/3oz/½ cup coarse semolina
2.5ml/½ tsp saffron strands
50g/2oz/⅓ cup sultanas (golden raisins)
90g/3½oz/½ cup sugar
300ml/½ pint/1¼ cups water
300ml/½ pint/1¼ cups full-fat (whole) milk

TO GARNISH

25g/1oz/¼ cup unsalted pistachio nut kernels
30ml/2 tbsp desiccated (dry unsweetened shredded) coconut
25g/1oz/¼ cup flaked (sliced) almonds

SOOJI KA HALVA
SEMOLINA DESSERT

This halva is eaten with pooris and potato curry (aloo bhujia) for breakfast all over Pakistan. It makes a delicious, sustaining brunch dish, but if you like you can just have the halva with some fresh cream for dessert or a snack.

1 Soak the pistachio nuts for the garnish in a small bowl of water for at least 3 hours, then peel them, thinly slice them and set them aside.

2 Meanwhile, melt the ghee in a medium pan over a medium heat. Add the cloves and cardamoms, reduce the heat, then add the semolina and stir-fry for 3–4 minutes, until the semolina turns a little darker.

3 Add the saffron, sultanas and the sugar. Mix in the water and milk and stir-fry continuously for about 10–15 minutes, until the semolina is soft. Add a drop of water if required.

4 Meanwhile, prepare the rest of the garnishes. Toast the coconut in a frying pan over a medium heat for 2–3 minutes, shaking it continuously, until it is golden brown. Toast the flaked almonds in the same way, until just golden.

5 Remove the semolina from the heat, transfer it to a serving dish and garnish with the pistachio nuts, coconut and flaked almonds.

SHEER KORMA
VERMICELLI DESSERT

Sheer korma, also known as seviyan, is a very popular Pakistani dessert that is a particular favourite (indeed, almost obligatory) at Eid. It can be served hot or cold – it's really a matter of personal choice. In most households, it is made in great quantities in a large punch bowl as it is quite liquid. In keeping with my mother's custom, in our household the bowl is placed as a centrepiece at the dining table and individual portions are offered in small dessert bowls to visiting friends and relations throughout the day.

SERVES 4

25g/1oz/¼ cup unsalted pistachio nut kernels, finely chopped
25g/1oz/¼ cup flaked (sliced) almonds
45ml/3 tbsp pure ghee
100g/4oz seviyan (see Cook's Tip)
900ml/1½ pints/3¾ cups full-fat (whole) milk
175ml/6fl oz/¾ cup evaporated milk or khoya
90g/3½oz/½ cup sugar
6 dates, stoned (pitted)

1 Soak the pistachio nuts in a small bowl of water for at least 3 hours, then peel them, thinly slice them and set them aside with the flaked almonds.

2 Melt the ghee in a large pan over a medium heat, then add the seviyan and reduce the heat to low. Fry until the seviyan turns golden brown – this happens very quickly so keep watching it and, if necessary, remove from the heat. Some bits may appear darker than the rest, but that is quite normal.

3 Add the milk and bring to boil slowly, taking care that it does not boil over. Add the evaporated milk, sugar and dates.

4 Simmer, uncovered, for about 10 minutes, stirring occasionally. When the consistency starts to thicken, pour it in a serving bowl and decorate with the chopped pistachios and the flaked almonds. Serve hot or cold in dessert bowls.

COOK'S TIP

Seviyan is a fine vermicelli that is only available in Asian stores. It is essential to use this type of vermicelli as the recipe will not work with any alternative.

GAJAR KA HALVA
CARROT DESSERT

I remember the time, before food processors were invented, when my mother (who always believed in producing dishes such as this in large quantities) made us children sit with a mound of carrots and a stainless-steel hand grater each. Grating all those carrots was rather a boring task and my sister and I used to get told off for chatting rather than working! This dish is worth the effort, however, and of course these days you can use a food processor to make life easier. I like to use pure ghee for this halva as it is rather special and tastes better than the vegetable one, but you can use the latter if you prefer. Decorated with warq and nuts, it makes a very impressive dinner-party dessert. It is best served warm, with fresh cream if desired, and can be made well in advance because it freezes very well.

SERVES 4

- 1.6kg/3½lb carrots
- 150g/5oz/10 tbsp pure ghee
- 600ml/1 pint/2½ cups full-fat (whole) milk
- 175ml/6fl oz/¾ cup evaporated milk or khoya (see Cook's Tip)
- seeds from 10 whole cardamoms, crushed
- 90–115g/3½–4½oz/½–⅔ cup sugar
- cream, to serve

TO GARNISH

- 25g/1oz/¼ cup unsalted pistachio nut kernels, chopped
- 25g/1oz/¼ cup flaked (sliced) almonds
- 2 leaves warq (edible silver leaf) (optional)

1 Wash, peel and grate the carrots, either using a box grater or a food processor.

2 Heat the ghee in a large, heavy pan. Add the grated carrots and stir-fry for 15–20 minutes, or until the moisture has evaporated and the carrots have darkened in colour.

3 Add the milk, evaporated milk or khoya, cardamoms and sugar to the carrots. Continue to stir-fry for a further 30–35 minutes, using semi-circular movements, until it is a rich brownish-red colour.

4 Transfer to a large shallow dish and garnish with the pistachio nuts, flaked almonds and warq. Serve warm or cold with some cream.

COOK'S TIP

Khoya is essentially milk that has been reduced down to a thick paste or solid. Making it is a lengthy process, so it is best just to buy khoya ready-prepared from an Asian store.

SHAHI TUKRAY
BREAD PUDDING – PAKISTANI-STYLE

The exact origins of this dish are slightly contentious, with some claiming it derives from an Ancient Egyptian bread pudding, others that it is Mughlai, and yet more people saying that it came from the days of the Raj. Its name translates as 'royal pieces', lending some credence to the idea that it may once have been enjoyed by Mughal emperors breaking their fast during Ramadan, and this tradition continues to this day since the dish features on many an iftar table. The original recipe does not contain egg, but this version does since it really works well.

SERVES 4

4 slices white bread
250ml/12fl oz/1½ cups full-fat (whole) milk
120ml/4fl oz/½ cup condensed milk
1 egg, beaten
2.5ml/½ tsp saffron strands
30ml/2 tbsp sugar
a large pinch of cardamom seeds
15ml/1 tbsp sultanas (golden raisins)
butter, for greasing
vegetable ghee, for shallow-frying
cream or crème fraîche, to serve

1 Cut the crusts off the bread and then slice the pieces either into squares, triangles or diamond shapes.

2 Whisk together the milk, condensed milk, beaten egg, saffron, sugar, cardamom seeds and sultanas in a bowl.

3 Lightly grease a 5cm/2in-deep oven dish with some butter. Preheat the oven to 180°C/350°F/Gas 4.

4 Heat the ghee in a wok or frying pan and fry the bread slices in batches until crisp and golden brown. Place these in the prepared dish, then pour the milk and egg mixture over the top of the bread.

5 Bake for 15–20 minutes, checking to see whether it is cooked by piercing the dessert with a knife. Cook for a further 5–7 minutes if necessary. Remove from the oven and serve warm with cream or crème fraîche.

SERVES 4

175g/6oz/1½ cups whole almonds
45ml/3 tbsp sugar
a pinch of saffron strands (optional)
600ml/1 pint/2½ cups semi-skimmed (low-fat) milk

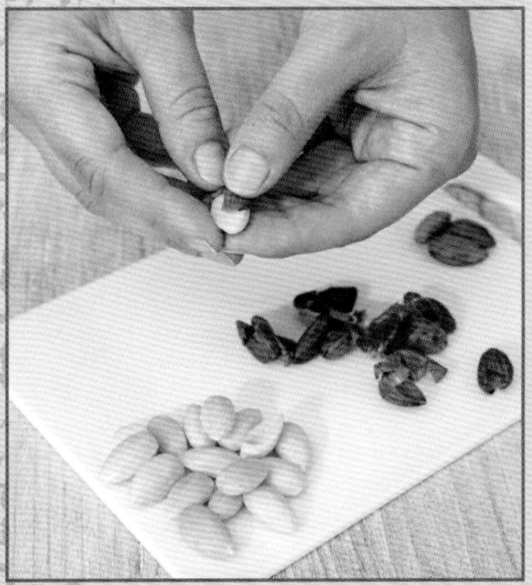

BADAM SHERBET
ALMOND SHERBET

You could use ready ground almonds to make this drink, but for a fuller and better flavour I suggest you soak whole almonds overnight then remove the skin and grind the nuts yourself. The drink is very nutritious and sustaining, making it an ideal beverage with which to break the daily fast of Ramadan or simply for a sultry day instead of food when you can't face a big meal.

1 Put the almonds in a large bowl with enough hot water to cover and leave to soak overnight or for a minimum of 3 hours.

2 Remove the skins from the almonds, then put them into a food processor and grind them to a smooth paste.

3 Add the sugar and blend again to combine. Add the saffron, if using, and the milk and blend once more to make a thick liquid.

4 Transfer the drink to a jug or pitcher and leave it to chill in the refrigerator. Stir well and serve cold.

GULAAB KAY SHEERAY KI LASSI
ROSE SYRUP LASSI

Drinks made with rose syrup are a must in the holy month of Ramadan in almost every Pakistani household. Lassis are refreshing and extremely thirst-quenching and can be made with water and ice, and/or with milk and yogurt, as here. Rose syrup is quite thick and sweet, with a delightful fragrance and the colour of red roses. You only need a few drops, as the flavour is very strong and a little goes a long way.

1 Whisk together the yogurt, milk and water in a large pitcher or jug; you can even put it through a blender to make it really light and frothy if you prefer.

2 Pour in the rose syrup and blend until it is well mixed together.

3 Pour the lassi into glasses and serve chilled, garnished with fresh mint leaves or edible rose petals.

SERVES 6

675g/1½lb/3 cups whole natural (plain) yogurt
250ml/8fl oz/1 cup full-fat (whole) milk
250ml/8fl oz/1 cup water
60ml/4 tbsp rose syrup
fresh mint leaves or edible rose petals, to garnish

COOK'S TIP

Rose syrup has a very intense flavour, and the strength can vary, so it is worth trying just a little to start with and adding more as necessary. If you don't like the flavour of rose, you can try orange blossom water or simply omit the flavouring altogether, if you prefer.

SERVES 2

300ml/½ pint/1¼ cups water
600ml/1 pint/2½ cups full-fat (whole) milk
1 medium stick of cinnamon
4–5 whole green cardamoms
3 bags strong black tea or chai
a large pinch of saffron strands
10ml/2 tsp sugar (optional)
nankhatai, to serve (see Cook's Tip)

ZAFRANI DOODH PATTI
SPICED SAFFRON TEA

An aromatic and delicately spiced tea, this makes a lovely end to a meal on a winter's day, and is especially beneficial if you have a cold. It is best cooked over the stove using half milk and half water, and tea leaves for preference, although you can use tea bags as here, for convenience. Traditionally, it is always served with sugar, but this is optional.

1 Put the water, milk, cinnamon and cardamoms in a pan and bring to the boil over a low-medium heat. Simmer for 5–7 minutes, making sure the liquid doesn't boil over.

2 Now add the tea bags and boil for a further 5–7 minutes or until the fluid has picked up the flavour and colour from the tea.

3 Add the saffron and sugar, if using. Blend everything together and pour it through a strainer into a tea pot. Serve hot with nankhatai.

COOK'S TIP

Nankhatai are a type of cookie that is popular in India and Pakistan. They are similar to shortbread, and contain flour, ghee, sugar, eggs, palm toddy and almonds. If you are unable to find them in an Asian store, then any simple cookie makes a great accompaniment to this aromatic tea.

NUTRITIONAL INFORMATION

p24 **POTATO AND CHICKPEA CHAAT** Energy 88kcal/373kJ; Protein 3g; Carbohydrate 19.2g, of which sugars 4.2g; Fat 0.6g, of which saturates 0.1g; Cholesterol 33mg; Calcium 72mg; Fibre 2.3g; Sodium 790mg.

p25 **POTATOES WITH CHICKPEAS AND PAAPRI** Energy 246kcal/1040kJ; Protein 9.4g; Carbohydrate 42.3g, of which sugars 9.1g; Fat 6.3g, of which saturates 1.3g; Cholesterol 33mg; Calcium 280mg; Fibre 6.1g; Sodium 1040mg.

p26 **SIMPLE SWEET-AND-SOUR CHAAT** Energy 206kcal/869kJ; Protein 7.8g; Carbohydrate 36.2g, of which sugars 5.2g; Fat 4.5g, of which saturates 0.8g; Cholesterol 33mg; Calcium 119mg; Fibre 6.8g; Sodium 758mg.

p27 **CHICKPEAS IN A SWEET-AND-SOUR SAUCE** Energy 144kcal/608kJ; Protein 6.7g; Carbohydrate 25.6g, of which sugars 10.3g; Fat 2.7g, of which saturates 0.3g; Cholesterol 8mg; Calcium 147mg; Fibre 5.9g; Sodium 684mg.

p28 **SPICED CHICKPEAS** Energy 207kcal/863kJ; Protein 6.1g; Carbohydrate 17.4g, of which sugars 4.5g; Fat 13.2g, of which saturates 1.5g; Cholesterol 0mg; Calcium 72mg; Fibre 5.3g; Sodium 643mg.

p29 **SPICED FRUIT SALAD** Energy 149kcal/632kJ; Protein 2.4g; Carbohydrate 35.3g, of which sugars 33.5g; Fat 0.9g, of which saturates 0.1g; Cholesterol 0mg; Calcium 63mg; Fibre 7.3g; Sodium 259mg.

p30 **SPICY POTATO FRIES** Energy 280kcal/1174kJ; Protein 3.4g; Carbohydrate 34g, of which sugars 1.3g; Fat 15.6g, of which saturates 5.8g; Cholesterol 0mg; Calcium 45mg; Fibre 2.8g; Sodium 311mg.

p31 **SPICY STIR-FRIED POTATOES** Energy 182kcal/762kJ; Protein 2.9g; Carbohydrate 24.6g, of which sugars 2g; Fat 8.8g, of which saturates 1.1g; Cholesterol 50mg; Calcium 40mg; Fibre 2.1g; Sodium 509mg.

p32 **POORIS WITH CHICKPEAS AND GINGER SAUCE** Energy 368kcal/1550kJ; Protein 11g; Carbohydrate 46.8g, of which sugars 3.9g; Fat 16.8g, of which saturates 2g; Cholesterol 0mg; Calcium 136mg; Fibre 7.6g; Sodium 498mg.

p34 **POTATO AND LENTIL PATTIES** Energy 353kcal/1492kJ; Protein 17.2g; Carbohydrate 56.2g, of which sugars 2.9g; Fat 8.2g, of which saturates 1.6g; Cholesterol 99mg; Calcium 123mg; Fibre 4.5g; Sodium 291mg.

p36 **BARBECUED CORN ON THE COB** Energy 255kcal/1070kJ; Protein 6.5g; Carbohydrate 29.8g, of which sugars 3.7g; Fat 13.6g, of which saturates 6.9g; Cholesterol 27mg; Calcium 147mg; Fibre 3.6g; Sodium 1064mg.

p37 **SWEET-AND-SOUR CHICKEN WINGS** Energy 560kcal/2345kJ; Protein 55.7g; Carbohydrate 10.1g, of which sugars 9g; Fat 33.5g, of which sat 9.3g; Cholesterol 240mg; Calcium 97mg; Fibre 1.4g; Sodium 784mg.

p38 **CHICKEN PAKORAS** Energy 301kcal/1258kJ; Protein 21.8g; Carbohydrate 20.3g, of which sugars 1g; Fat 15.2g, of which saturates 1.9g; Cholesterol 26mg; Calcium 178mg; Fibre 0.4g; Sodium 611mg.

p44 **TIGER PRAWNS WITH SHALLOTS AND PEPPERS** Energy 223kcal/922kJ; Protein 13.1g; Carbohydrate 2.9g, of which sugars 2.8g; Fat 18.5g, of which saturates 2.2g; Cholesterol 65mg; Calcium 219mg; Fibre 1.3g; Sodium 1927mg.

p45 **GRILLED GARLIC KING PRAWNS** Energy 61kcal/258kJ; Protein 12.4g; Carbohydrate 0.3g, of which sugars 0.2g; Fat 1.5g, of which saturates 0.3g; Cholesterol 65mg; Calcium 252mg; Fibre 0.5g; Sodium 2416mg.

p46 **CRISPY SPICY PRAWNS** Energy 226kcal/944kJ; Protein 13.4g; Carbohydrate 16.7g, of which sugars 2.9g; Fat 12.1g, of which saturates 1.7g; Cholesterol 142mg; Calcium 100mg; Fibre 0.1g; Sodium 1523mg.

p48 **TANDOORI-STYLE PRAWNS** Energy 319kcal/1332kJ; Protein 12.3g; Carbohydrate 2.6g, of which sugars 2g; Fat 29.1g, of which saturates 15.2g; Cholesterol 202mg; Calcium 180mg; Fibre 0.9g; Sodium 799mg.

p50 **LAHORI FRIED FISH** Energy 251kcal/1049kJ; Protein 18.2g; Carbohydrate 18.6g, of which sugars 0.1g; Fat 12.2g, of which saturates 1.5g; Cholesterol 14mg; Calcium 260mg; Fibre 0.8g; Sodium 516mg.

p52 **CHILLI-FRIED COD** Energy 221kcal/922kJ; Protein 17.7g; Carbohydrate 11.9g, of which sugars 4g; Fat 12.5g, of which saturates 1.5g; Cholesterol 40mg; Calcium 230mg; Fibre 1.7g; Sodium 263mg.

p58 **CLEAR CHICKEN AND VEGETABLE CONSOMMÉ** Energy 143kcal/606kJ; Protein 30.7g; Carbohydrate 2.5g, of which sugars 2.4g; Fat 1.2g, of which saturates 0.3g; Cholesterol 70mg; Calcium 12mg; Fibre 0.9g; Sodium 1260mg.

p60 **TANDOORI CHICKEN** Energy 428kcal/1794kJ; Protein 54.8g; Carbohydrate 4g, of which sugars 2g; Fat 21.6g, of which saturates 6.6g; Cholesterol 240mg; Calcium 116mg; Fibre 0g; Sodium 1180mg.

p62 **POTATO AND LEMON CHICKEN** Energy 319kcal/1330kJ; Protein 19.7g; Carbohydrate 14.9g, of which sugars 3.7g; Fat 20.5g, of which saturates 2.6g; Cholesterol 77mg; Calcium 12mg; Fibre 1.9g; Sodium 55mg.

p64 **LAHORI CHICKEN** Energy 334kcal/1389kJ; Protein 19.9g; Carbohydrate 9.2g, of which sugars 8.3g; Fat 24.5g, of which saturates 4.5g; Cholesterol 53mg; Calcium 27mg; Fibre 3.4g; Sodium 310mg.

p66 **CHICKEN DOPIAZA** Energy 529kcal/2207kJ; Protein 53.7g; Carbohydrate 17.8g, of which sugars 12.6g; Fat 27.5g, of which saturates 3.5g; Cholesterol 149mg; Calcium 67mg; Fibre 4.2g; Sodium 871mg.

p68 **FRIED MINCED CHICKEN** Energy 304kcal/1269kJ; Protein 29.1g; Carbohydrate 12.1g, of which sugars 10.9g; Fat 15.7g, of which saturates 2.2g; Cholesterol 79mg; Calcium 30mg; Fibre 4.1g; Sodium 819mg.

p70 **CHICKEN WITH SPINACH** Energy 307kcal/1275kJ; Protein 22.3g; Carbohydrate 6.6g, of which sugars 4.9g; Fat 21.4g, of which saturates 2.7g; Cholesterol 55mg; Calcium 128mg; Fibre 3.3g; Sodium 962mg.

p72 **CHICKEN WITH GREEN SPICES** Energy 226kcal/942kJ; Protein 19.4g; Carbohydrate 3.8g, of which sugars 3.7g; Fat 14.9g, of which saturates 2g; Cholesterol 53mg; Calcium 26mg; Fibre 1.2g; Sodium 790mg.

p74 **PAKISTANI FRIED CHICKEN** Energy 385kcal/1612kJ; Protein 48g; Carbohydrate 2.8g, of which sugars 2.6g; Fat 20.3g, of which saturates 2.7g; Cholesterol 132mg; Calcium 76mg; Fibre 0g; Sodium 624mg.

p76 **MASALA CREAMY CHICKEN** Energy 507kcal/2102kJ; Protein 24.5g; Carbohydrate 9.8g, of which sugars 7.3g; Fat 41.5g, of which saturates 18.9g; Cholesterol 122mg; Calcium 73mg; Fibre 1.9g; Sodium 182mg.

p78 **KASHMIRI CHICKEN WITH DRIED FRUITS** Energy 321kcal/1337kJ; Protein 21.3g; Carbohydrate 13.2g, of which sugars 10.7g; Fat 20.7g, of which saturates 6.1g; Cholesterol 70mg; Calcium 53mg; Fibre 3g; Sodium 558mg.

p80 **CHICKEN WITH CHICKPEAS** Energy 295kcal/1230kJ; Protein 21.1g; Carbohydrate 12.3g, of which sugars 6.5g; Fat 18.3g, of which saturates 2.3g; Cholesterol 53mg; Calcium 37mg; Fibre 3.3g; Sodium 613mg.

p82 **LAHORI STEAMED CHICKEN** Energy 517kcal/2150kJ; Protein 52.6g; Carbohydrate 0.6g, of which sugars 0.6g; Fat 37.4g, of which sat 7.9g; Cholesterol 213mg; Calcium 120mg; Fibre 0g; Sodium 229mg.

p84 **MALAI CHICKEN TIKKA** Energy 295kcal/1227kJ; Protein 23.7g; Carbohydrate 0.7g, of which sugars 0.7g; Fat 22g, of which saturates 10.7g; Cholesterol 108mg; Calcium 10mg; Fibre 0.2g; Sodium 918mg.

p86 **CHICKEN COOKED WITH PICKLING SPICES** Energy 217kcal/904kJ; Protein 23.8g; Carbohydrate 3.8g, of which sugars 2.2g; Fat 12.5g, of which saturates 1.7g; Cholesterol 66mg; Calcium 169mg; Fibre 1g; Sodium 552mg.

p88 **KAT-A-KAT CHICKEN** Energy 319kcal/1329kJ; Protein 31.5g; Carbohydrate 7.7g, of which sugars 5.9g; Fat 18.2g, of which saturates 2.4g; Cholesterol 88mg; Calcium 40mg; Fibre 1.9g; Sodium 85mg.

p94 **MINCED LAMB WITH FRESH FENUGREEK** Energy 332kcal/1382kJ; Protein 26.8g; Carbohydrate 8.6g, of which sugars 6.9g; Fat 21.4g, of which saturates 5.7g; Cholesterol 93mg; Calcium 40mg; Fibre 2.6g; Sodium 589mg.

p96 **LAMB PASANDA** Energy 318kcal/1322kJ; Protein 26.3g; Carbohydrate 8.5g, of which sugars 6.6g; Fat 20.1g, of which saturates 6.5g; Cholesterol 84mg; Calcium 89mg; Fibre 1.4g; Sodium 105mg.

p98 **MUTTON COOKED WITH LENTILS** Energy 649kcal/2721kJ; Protein 43.9g; Carbohydrate 53.8g, of which sugars 6.3g; Fat 30.2g, of which saturates 6.4g; Cholesterol 83mg; Calcium 76mg; Fibre 7g; Sodium 849mg.

p100 **LAMB BHUNA** Energy 388kcal/1610kJ; Protein 25.3g; Carbohydrate 13.7g, of which sugars 11g; Fat 26.1g, of which saturates 6g; Cholesterol 83mg; Calcium 66mg; Fibre 3.5g; Sodium 586mg.

p102 **LAMB AND CAULIFLOWER CURRY WITH PEPPERS** Energy 445kcal/1848kJ; Protein 28.6g; Carbohydrate 14.9g, of which sugars 12.4g; Fat 30.5g, of which saturates 6.6g; Cholesterol 83mg; Calcium 63mg; Fibre 6g; Sodium 95mg.

p104 **SLOW-COOKED MUTTON STEW** Energy 609kcal/2535kJ; Protein 52.7g; Carbohydrate 12.6g, of which sugars 5.2g; Fat 39g, of which saturates 17.8g; Cholesterol 185mg; Calcium 78mg; Fibre 1.7g; Sodium 1167mg.

p106 **MUTTON CURRY WITH KEWRA WATER** Energy 324kcal/1337kJ; Protein 2.3g; Carbohydrate 10.3g, of which sugars 7.7g; Fat 30.8g, of which saturates 9.8g; Cholesterol 0mg; Calcium 54mg; Fibre 2.8g; Sodium 506mg.

p108 **POTATOES WITH MUTTON** Energy 542kcal/2252kJ; Protein 20.8g; Carbohydrate 27.7g, of which sugars 10.3g; Fat 39.5g, of which saturates 11.8g; Cholesterol 93mg; Calcium 54mg; Fibre 4.6g; Sodium 809mg.

p110 **MASHED MUTTON WITH CRUSHED WHEAT AND OATS** Energy 647kcal/2694kJ; Protein 16.2g; Carbohydrate 62.7g, of which sugars 13.3g; Fat 38.3g, of which saturates 18g; Cholesterol 71mg; Calcium 190mg; Fibre 6.1g; Sodium 1042mg.

p112 **SPICED LAMB CHOPS** Energy 742kcal/3081kJ; Protein 53.3g; Carbohydrate 6.2g, of which sugars 4.4g; Fat 56.2g, of which saturates 21.9g; Cholesterol 194mg; Calcium 66mg; Fibre 1.4g; Sodium 653mg.

p114 **CHAPLEE KEBABS** Energy 340kcal/1415kJ; Protein 24.3g; Carbohydrate 4.5g, of which sugars 1.7g; Fat 25.1g, of which saturates 8.5g; Cholesterol 144mg; Calcium 42mg; Fibre 1g; Sodium 595mg.

p116 **SIMPLE MINCED MUTTON KEBABS** Energy 390kcal/1619kJ; Protein 25g; Carbohydrate 10.3g, of which sugars 5.1g; Fat 27.9g, of which saturates 8.8g; Cholesterol 144mg; Calcium 57mg; Fibre 1.8g; Sodium 628mg.

p118 **TRADITIONAL SEEKH KEBABS** Energy 237kcal/989kJ; Protein 22.2g; Carbohydrate 3.5g, of which sugars 2.6g; Fat 15.1g, of which saturates 7g; Cholesterol 87mg; Calcium 31mg; Fibre 0.7g; Sodium 80mg.

p120 **MASALA MINCED MUTTON KEBAB ROLLS** Energy 375kcal/1563kJ; Protein 27g; Carbohydrate 7.1g, of which sugars 0.6g; Fat 26.8g, of which saturates 9.3g; Cholesterol 154mg; Calcium 46mg; Fibre 0.4g; Sodium 915mg.

p122 **MINCED LAMB PATTIES IN PUFF PASTRY** Energy 787kcal/3279kJ; Protein 33.5g; Carbohydrate 52.7g, of which sugars 6.4g; Fat 50.6g, of which saturates 19.6g; Cholesterol 164mg; Calcium 109mg; Fibre 1.4g; Sodium 970mg.

p124 **MARINATED GRILLED LAMB** Energy 208kcal/868kJ; Protein 23.6g; Carbohydrate 1.6g, of which sugars 1.6g; Fat 11.9g, of which saturates 4.3g; Cholesterol 83mg; Calcium 35mg; Fibre 0g; Sodium 825mg.

p126 **GRILLED MINCED MUTTON** Energy 378kcal/1572kJ; Protein 25.4g; Carbohydrate 7g, of which sugars 5.3g; Fat 27.9g, of which saturates 9.1g; Cholesterol 96mg; Calcium 54mg; Fibre 1.4g; Sodium 586mg.

p128 **POTATO AND MUTTON CUTLETS** Energy 548kcal/2279kJ; Protein 27.1g; Carbohydrate 23.3g, of which sugars 3.8g; Fat 39.2g, of which saturates 10.4g; Cholesterol 117mg; Calcium 53mg; Fibre 1.9g; Sodium 928mg.

p130 **AROMATIC MUTTON STEW** Energy 393kcal/1636kJ; Protein 27.4g; Carbohydrate 10.8g, of which sugars 9.1g; Fat 27.1g, of which saturates 6.4g; Cholesterol 93mg; Calcium 55mg; Fibre 2.9g; Sodium 842mg.

p132 **LAMB NEHARI** Energy 641kcal/2665kJ; Protein 36.9g; Carbohydrate 22.5g, of which sugars 5.6g; Fat 45.4g, of which saturates 10.7g; Cholesterol 131mg; Calcium 56mg; Fibre 2.5g; Sodium 857mg.

p134 **FRIED MUTTON LIVER** Energy 380kcal/1580kJ; Protein 26.4g; Carbohydrate 6.3g, of which sugars 4.6g; Fat 27.9g, of which saturates 4.5g; Cholesterol 538mg; Calcium 28mg; Fibre 1.4g; Sodium 95mg.

p136 **BEEF GOLA KEBABS** Energy 302kcal/1261kJ; Protein 29.2g; Carbohydrate 9.7g, of which sugars 2.7g; Fat 16.5g, of which saturates 3.5g; Cholesterol 73mg; Calcium 16mg; Fibre 0.9g; Sodium 646mg.

p138 **SPICED BEEF PATTIES** Energy 301kcal/1268kJ; Protein 38g; Carbohydrate 21.3g, of which sugars 3.9g; Fat 7.6g, of which saturates 2.7g; Cholesterol 130mg; Calcium 70mg; Fibre 2.9g; Sodium 851mg.

p144 **SPICY PAKISTANI-STYLE OMELETTE** Energy 284kcal/1177kJ; Protein 14.1g; Carbohydrate 5.5g, of which sugars 4.4g; Fat 23g, of which saturates 4.7g; Cholesterol 404mg; Calcium 76mg; Fibre 1.6g; Sodium 399mg.

p146 **MASALA POTATOES AND AUBERGINES** Energy 243kcal/1015kJ; Protein 6.1g; Carbohydrate 27.2g, of which sugars 10.3g; Fat 13g, of which saturates 1.6g; Cholesterol 21mg; Calcium 54mg; Fibre 8.4g; Sodium 91mg.

p148 **POTATO CURRY WITH CURRY LEAVES** Energy 199kcal/831kJ; Protein 2.8g; Carbohydrate 22.6g, of which sugars 6g; Fat 11.5g, of which saturates 1.4g; Cholesterol 33mg; Calcium 27mg; Fibre 2.7g; Sodium 506mg.

p149 **FRIED CAULIFLOWER** Energy 171kcal/706kJ; Protein 5g; Carbohydrate 10.5g, of which sugars 8.9g; Fat 12.3g, of which saturates 1.6g; Cholesterol 0mg; Calcium 38mg; Fibre 4.5g; Sodium 210mg.

p150 **CHICKPEAS AND SPINACH** Energy 103kcal/430kJ; Protein 3.2g; Carbohydrate 8.1g, of which sugars 2.5g; Fat 6.7g, of which saturates 0.9g; Cholesterol 0mg; Calcium 48mg; Fibre 2.5g; Sodium 226mg.

p152 **OKRA WITH TOMATOES** Energy 126kcal/522kJ; Protein 2.1g; Carbohydrate 3.4g, of which sugars 3g; Fat 11.8g, of which saturates 1.5g; Cholesterol 0mg; Calcium 112mg; Fibre 4g; Sodium 499mg.

p154 **CLASSIC TARKA DAAL** Energy 338kcal/1428kJ; Protein 21.1g; Carbohydrate 51.8g, of which sugars 4.9g; Fat 7g, of which saturates 0.9g; Cholesterol 0mg; Calcium 148mg; Fibre 6.5g; Sodium 34mg.

p156 **SPICED URID TARKA DAAL** Energy 309kcal/1295kJ; Protein 13.7g; Carbohydrate 33.2g, of which sugars 2.5g; Fat 14.4g, of which saturates 7.7g; Cholesterol 16mg; Calcium 35mg; Fibre 4g; Sodium 558mg.

p158 **CREAMY BLACK LENTIL DAAL** Energy 665kcal/2782kJ; Protein 26.7g; Carbohydrate 60.8g, of which sugars 9.8g; Fat 37.1g, of which saturates 16.6g; Cholesterol 61mg; Calcium 223mg; Fibre 16.9g; Sodium 388mg.

p164 **VEGETABLE RICE** Energy 406kcal/1689kJ; Protein 6.8g; Carbohydrate 67.1g, of which sugars 6.5g; Fat 11.9g, of which saturates 5.6g; Cholesterol 0mg; Calcium 42mg; Fibre 2.2g; Sodium 506mg.

p165 **CHICKPEA RICE** Energy 414kcal/1731kJ; Protein 10.4g; Carbohydrate 70.7g, of which sugars 0.3g; Fat 9.8g, of which saturates 3.8g; Cholesterol 0mg; Calcium 44mg; Fibre 3.7g; Sodium 886mg.

p166 **SPICY PRAWN RICE** Energy 368kcal/1533kJ; Protein 16.2g; Carbohydrate 48g, of which sugars 7.7g; Fat 12.2g, of which saturates 1.5g; Cholesterol 140mg; Calcium 82mg; Fibre 2.9g; Sodium 1298mg.

p168 **CHICKEN TIKKA BIRYANI** Energy 523kcal/2184kJ; Protein 27.9g; Carbohydrate 64.9g, of which sugars 3.9g; Fat 16.6g, of which saturates 10.3g; Cholesterol 103mg; Calcium 56mg; Fibre 0.9g; Sodium 64mg.

p170 **SINDHI CHICKEN BIRYANI** Energy 875kcal/3655kJ; Protein 41.4g; Carbohydrate 109.6g, of which sugars 15.9g; Fat 30.3g, of which saturates 14.1g; Cholesterol 112mg; Calcium 100mg; Fibre 5.5g; Sodium 114mg.

p172 **MUTTON BIRYANI** Energy 1029kcal/4285kJ; Protein 51.1g; Carbohydrate 102g, of which sugars 2.3g; Fat 45.5g, of which saturates 21g; Cholesterol 148mg; Calcium 96mg; Fibre 0g; Sodium 159mg.

p174 **GREEN PEA PULAO RICE** Energy 277kcal/1154kJ; Protein 5g; Carbohydrate 44.3g, of which sugars 2.4g; Fat 8.7g, of which saturates 3.1g; Cholesterol 0mg; Calcium 22mg; Fibre 1.5g; Sodium 1mg.

p176 **PUNJABI-STYLE CHOPS PULAO** Energy 808kcal/3372kJ; Protein 45.5g; Carbohydrate 86.9g, of which sugars 5.3g; Fat 30.6g, of which saturates 14.2g; Cholesterol 120mg; Calcium 90mg; Fibre 1.4g; Sodium 849mg.

p178 **SPICED POTATO-FILLED FLAKY BREAD** Energy 258kcal/1089kJ; Protein 7.7g; Carbohydrate 41g, of which sugars 1.9g; Fat 8.2g, of which saturates 1g; Cholesterol 9mg; Calcium 25mg; Fibre 7.2g; Sodium 128mg.

p180 **TANDOORI LEAVENED BREAD** Energy 258kcal/1089kJ; Protein 7.7g; Carbohydrate 41g, of which sugars 1.9g; Fat 8.2g, of which saturates 1g; Cholesterol 9mg; Calcium 25mg; Fibre 7.2g; Sodium 128mg.

p182 **DATE AND TAMARIND CHUTNEY** (Serves 12) Energy 62kcal/263kJ; Protein 0.6g; Carbohydrate 15.7g, of which sugars 15.7g; Fat 0g, of which saturates 0g; Cholesterol 0mg; Calcium 10mg; Fibre 1g; Sodium 166mg.

p183 **MINT AND RAW MANGO CHUTNEY** Energy 32kcal/136kJ; Protein 0.8g; Carbohydrate 7.3g, of which sugars 6.5g; Fat 0.2g, of which saturates 0g; Cholesterol 0mg; Calcium 31mg; Fibre 1.3g; Sodium 248mg.

p188 **SWEET SAFFRON RICE** Energy 394kcal/1665kJ; Protein 4.1g; Carbohydrate 96.5g, of which sugars 56.6g; Fat 0.3g, of which saturates 0g; Cholesterol 0mg; Calcium 28mg; Fibre 0.2g; Sodium 4mg.

p190 **MANGO RICE PUDDING** Energy 503kcal/2110kJ; Protein 14.1g; Carbohydrate 64.4g, of which sugars 48.9g; Fat 22.3g, of which saturates 10.2g; Cholesterol 52mg; Calcium 380mg; Fibre 2.6g; Sodium 171mg.

p191 **SEMOLINA DESSERT** Energy 386kcal/1620kJ; Protein 4.9g; Carbohydrate 50.3g, of which sugars 35.8g; Fat 19.8g, of which saturates 12.7g; Cholesterol 57mg; Calcium 101mg; Fibre 0.9g; Sodium 47mg.

p192 **VERMICELLI DESSERT** Energy 593kcal/2477kJ; Protein 16.3g; Carbohydrate 58.9g, of which sugars 38.9g; Fat 33.4g, of which saturates 16.4g; Cholesterol 78mg; Calcium 413mg; Fibre 0.8g; Sodium 261mg.

p194 **CARROT DESSERT** Energy 731kcal/3036kJ; Protein 11g; Carbohydrate 66g, of which sugars 64g; Fat 48.6g, of which saturates 31.3g; Cholesterol 141mg; Calcium 399mg; Fibre 12.8g; Sodium 263mg.

p196 **BREAD PUDDING – PAKISTANI-STYLE** Energy 252kcal/1064kJ; Protein 8.9g; Carbohydrate 39.3g, of which sugars 26.7g; Fat 7.7g, of which saturates 4.1g; Cholesterol 77mg; Calcium 202mg; Fibre 0.7g; Sodium 233mg.

p197 **ALMOND SHERBET** Energy 378kcal/1574kJ; Protein 14.2g; Carbohydrate 21.8g, of which sugars 20.6g; Fat 26.8g, of which saturates 3.6g; Cholesterol 11mg; Calcium 276mg; Fibre 0g; Sodium 85mg.p198

p198 **ROSE SYRUP LASSI** Energy 114kcal/483kJ; Protein 6.7g; Carbohydrate 16.6g, of which sugars 16.6g; Fat 2.8g, of which saturates 1.7g; Cholesterol 7mg; Calcium 228mg; Fibre 0g; Sodium 122mg.

p199 **SPICED SAFFRON TEA** Energy 198kcal/828kJ; Protein 9.6g; Carbohydrate 14.4g, of which sugars 14.4g; Fat 11.7g, of which saturates 7.1g; Cholesterol 42mg; Calcium 330mg; Fibre 0g; Sodium 165mg.

INDEX

N

O

P

Q

R

S

T

V

W

Y

Z

BISMILLAH-HIR-RAHMAN-NIR-RAHEEM

For my grandchildren Zahra, Gibrael, Mikael, Azlan and Rafael, all my love and prayers. My special thanks to my husband Arif for his cooperation and continued support in everything I do.

This edition is published by Lorenz Books, an imprint of Anness Publishing Ltd
info@anness.com; www.lorenzbooks.com; www.annesspublishing.com

If you like the images in this book and would like to investigate using them for publishing, promotions or advertising, please visit our website www.practicalpictures.com for more information.

Publisher: Joanna Lorenz
Project Editor: Lucy Doncaster
Photographer: Jon Whitaker
Designer: Simon Daley
Home Economist: Emily Jonzen
Prop Stylist: Jenny Iggleden
Illustrator: Georgie Fearns

Picture credits: Alamy 8, 9t, 9br, 10t, 10bl, 12,14bl, 23, 43, 57, 93, 143, 163, 187; iStock 7, 9bl, 9cr, 11, 13, 17, 19, 200–1.
Author picture on cover: Chris Johnson at Image Studio in Chislehurst

RECIPE NOTES

- Bracketed terms are intended for American readers. For all recipes, quantities are given in both metric and imperial measures and, where appropriate, in standard cups and spoons. Follow one set of measures, but not a mixture, because they are not interchangeable.
- Standard spoon and cup measures are level. 1 tsp = 5ml, 1 tbsp = 15ml, 1 cup = 250ml/8fl oz. Australian standard tablespoons are 20ml. Australian readers should use 3 tsp in place of 1 tbsp for measuring small quantities.
- American pints are 16fl oz/2 cups. American readers should use 20fl oz/2.5 cups in place of 1 pint when measuring liquids.
- Oven temperatures are for conventional ovens. When using a fan oven, the temperature will probably need to be reduced by about 10–20°C/20–40°F – check with your manufacturer's instruction book for guidance.
- The nutritional analysis for each recipe is calculated per portion (i.e. serving or item), unless otherwise stated. If the recipe gives a range, such as Serves 4–6, then the analysis will be for the smaller portion size, ie 6 servings. The analysis does not include optional ingredients.
- Medium (US large) eggs are used unless otherwise stated.